DRAMATICA®
FOR
SCREENWRITERS™

How to get the most out of Dramatica Pro
while writing or rewriting a Screenplay

by
Armando Saldaña Mora

Based on a theory developed by
Melanie Anne Phillips and Chris Huntley

Write Brothers®

P   O   D

ISBN 0-918973-03-1

ACKNOWLEDGMENTS

To my wife, Citlalli, and my daughter, Nicté, two very smart and courageous women, who not only gave me their support throughout my career as a writer, but also the determination to learn—and the assistance to understand—this New Theory of Story called Dramatica.

To Melanie Anne Phillips and Chris Huntley, another pair of extremely bright and brave people. They discovered and developed this amazing system that allowed me to write dozens and dozens of stories.

And, of course, to all Dramatica users around the world who ultimately made me comprehend and understand how to write and create with Dramatica. To those who doubted it and discussed it; to those who made me think and rethink its theory and applications; to those who gave me challenged my perspective until I understood it well enough to write what's in these pages.

To all those cited above, this book is dedicated.

—Armando Saldaña Mora

EDITOR'S NOTE

When I decided it was time to have someone right a practical, "how to" book on Dramatica I immediately thought of Armando. I wanted someone familiar with Dramatica who also had real world experience writing scripts. I needed someone with a track record as an effective teacher. I also thought it should be written by someone other than the authors of the book, **Dramatica: A New Theory of Story.** *Armando was a rare combination of all these qualities.*

I originally wanted a general, how to use Dramatica book for all writers: novelists, playwrights, creative writers, and screenwriters. It quickly became clear that was too much to cover in a single book. For that reason we decided to narrow the scope to screenwriting. Armando took Dramatica concepts and pushed them to their limits. The result is a book I never would have imagined. **Dramatica for Screenwriters** *successfully complements the Dramatica theory book and software by showing how to get the best out of both. Working with him on this book has been a great pleasure.*

I would like to thank all those who helped make this book possible. Thanks to the members of the Dramatica Listserv, particularly list manager and host, Bill Schindler, without whom Armando would not have had a venue for the original "Instant Dramatica." Special thanks to Julia Mozingo, Prish Fraker, Carl Weaver, Joy A. Higgins, Sandy Stone, Barbara Schiffman, and Key Payton for their editorial and proofing suggestions. And thanks to all you Dramatica users whose continued interest provided the motivation for the creation of this book.

Chris Huntley
Editor

Contents

INTRODUCTION

WHAT TO EXPECT FROM READING THIS BOOK

THE REAL LOWDOWN ON THIS BOOK

Are you afraid this may be a "Dramatica For Dimwits" manual?
Don't worry—it's not.
Mostly because you're not a dimwit (look, you bought the book!).
But also because Dramatica (the theory) and Dramatica® Pro (the software)
are deep and expansive tools for creative writing. So this book is for creative types
(or for those who want help to be), and it takes a very creative approach. It merges
software reference, inspirational exercises, and literary theory. It is part *Dramatica
Query System Quick Guide*, part *"What Would Happen If…?"* and part Aristotle's
Poetics.

So don't expect the instructions to be as concrete as *"Press the ENTER key…"*
or *"Type C:/Setup…"* Rather, expect them to be as imaginative as: *"Picture your
characters as people you know…"* or *"Think of several possibilities for the scene that
illustrates…"*

This book asks you to be inventive, productive, inspired, original, and much
more. It coaches you through one screenwriter's way of understanding Dramatica's
features and, if you stick with it all the way through, it equips you to use Dramatica
to write numerous well-developed and entertaining stories for the screen.

Isn't that what you really want?

How To Use This Book

Dramatica for Screenwriters is a companion piece to the Dramatica® Pro
software. Specifically, the book works best with version Dramatica® Pro 4. Though
there are many references to specific features and reports unique to version 4,
most examples, tips, and exercises apply to all versions of Dramatica, and often, to
screenwriting in general. A passing familiarity with Dramatica's basic terminology is
recommended.

Who This Book Is For

Dramatica for Screenwriters focuses on the practical application of Dramatica®
Pro for the development, writing, and rewriting of motion picture screenplays. This

book is for everyone involved in developing a script. This includes writers, script doctors, story editors, development executives, producers, directors, and anyone else interested enough in the script to take part in improving its character depth, entertainment value, meaningfulness, and satisfying completeness.

What This Book Is Not

Though this book is chock-full of general purpose advice on writing, it is **not** your basic "How to Write a Screenplay" reference book. *Dramatica for Screenwriters* does not describe proper script format, nor does it tell you how to sell your script or get an agent. Dozens of fine books on those subjects are already available online or in bookstores. This book focuses strictly on how to use the profound writing tool called Dramatica to develop great stories for the screen.

What If You Don't Have Dramatica® Pro?

If you don't have Dramatica® Pro software, but you do write screenplays or other forms of fiction, you may find *Dramatica for Screenwriters* loaded with useful information and ideas. Like the Dramatica Theory, this book offers concepts that numerous professional fiction writers now praise as the most insightful and biggest paradigm shift they have ever learned, regardless of their previous literary training.

Dramatica Terminology

Dramatica is filled with specific terminology. Some of it is unique to Dramatica. Most are familiar terms used in specific, non-traditional ways. Over the years there have been changes to some of the Dramatica terminology. If you are new to Dramatica, you won't notice these changes. If you're a longtime Dramatica user, a list of the changes appear on the next page.

In addition to the terminology, there are four acronyms frequently used in this book. They are:

- OS—Overall Story, the "big picture" part of your story which typically involves a Story Goal and the efforts of the characters to achieve it.

- MC—Main Character, the character through whose eyes the audience experiences the story.

- IC—Impact Character, the character who holds an alternative perspective to that of the MC.

- SS—Subjective Story (also known as M/I, MC/IC, Main Character v. Impact Character Story), the key relationship explored in the story.

Dramatica Terminology changes since its first Introduction

Current Term	Original Term
Overall Story	Objective Story
Impact Character	Obstacle Character
Main vs. Impact	Subjective Story*
Throughline**	Domain
Situation	Universe
Activity	Physics
Fixed Attitude	Mind
Manipulation	Psychology
How Things Are Changing	Progress
Gathering Information	Learning
Developing A Plan	Conceptualizing
Conceiving An Idea	Conceiving
Playing A Role	Being
Changing One's Nature	Becoming
Memories	Memory
Impulsive Responses	Preconscious
Contemplation	Conscious
Innermost Desires	Subconscious
Symptom [*element*]	Focus [*element*]
Response [*element*]	Direction [*element*]
Issue	Range
Benchmark	Stipulation
Main Character Growth	Main Character Direction
Main Character Problem-Solving Technique	Main Character Mental Sex*
Logical / Linear	Male* [*Mental Sex*]
Intuitive / Holistic	Female* [*Mental Sex*]
Story Driver	Story Work
Story Point	Appreciation

The original term is used in this book in lieu of the new term.

**For simplicity's sake, Throughline is used in place of Domain in Dramatica® Pro 4 even though they aren't truly the same . See the Dramatica Dictionary at www.dramatica.com for further clarification.*

Brief definitions for many of these terms are in the appendix at the back of this book. Longer definitions may be found online at Dramatica.com, in Dramatica® Pro's online dictionary, and in the Dramatica theory book, *Dramatica: A New Theory of Story* (10th edition).

SECTION I

WHAT DRAMATICA OFFERS THE SCREENWRITER

1

THE DRAMATICA PHILOSOPHY

Okay, forget the philosophy. Let me tell you what's really on your mind:

Does Dramatica guarantee I'll sell my screenplay?

and…

Should I obey and comply with all Dramatica rules?

Am I right? Are those the questions burning holes in the brain of every Dramatica user, or what?

Long ago, when I started with the Dramatica software, I wondered, *"Should I obey and comply with all Dramatica rules?"* and *"Does Dramatica guarantee I'll sell my screenplay?"* I was ignorant of several truths about the art of selling a screenplay. Since then I've learned a lot. Here's what I found out:

- Every single script I write competes against 39,999 other scripts written each year. Even the most meager independent filmmaker gets piles and piles of new stories to read. Agents get them by the ton. Studios get them in truckloads. In a nutshell:

> **THE SCREENPLAY MARKET HAS REACHED A POINT WHERE WRITING A GOOD SCREENPLAY IS JUST NOT ENOUGH.**

- No matter how much I polish a script, somebody will ask me to rewrite it. That's the nature of screenwriting. An optioned script goes through a dozen drafts before it's sold. Once it's sold, it goes through two dozen more rewrites before it even sees the light of pre-production. My conclusion is this:

> **IN THE SCREENWRITING BUSINESS, REWRITING IS AT LEAST, IF NOT MORE, ESSENTIAL THAN WRITING.**

- Every agent, producer, or director who doesn't already know me opens my script, instinctively looks for the writer's name on the cover page and thinks: *Who the heck is this guy? Does he even know what he's doing? What if he's an amateur? I can't waste my time with amateurish scripts! I don't have time for this!* So, without reading anything but my name, they throw my manuscript into the "Read Later" pile—where it gathers dust for a thousand years. Here's the catch-22:

> **A SCREENWRITER HAS TO SHOW DEEP KNOWLEDGE AND CRAFT EXPERTISE JUST TO EARN THE HONOR OF BEING READ.**

- The few times I got past the reading stage and got a meeting with an agent/producer/director, I find out they don't have much interest in discussing my story. They have lots of interest in discussing the potential stories I could write for them: *"Can you write maybe a light, romantic comedy?"* or *"Can you write a vehicle for this young actor?"* I found that there is a "screenwriters A-list." It consists of writers who can tackle any idea, who can handle and deliver all the potential projects pretty much as requested. So the moral of the story is:

> **IN THIS SWARMING, OVERFLOWING MARKET OF SPEC SUBMISSIONS, SCREENPLAYS HAVE BECOME CHEAP—WHILE SCREENWRITERS (GOOD ONES, WHO CONSISTENTLY KNOW WHAT THEY'RE DOING) HAVE BECOME PRIZED CITIZENS.**

So I wrestled with these colossal truths of the trade while also trying to understand how to write with Dramatica—all the time tortured by an underlying doubt: *Does Dramatica guarantee I'll sell my screenplay?*

Well sure, Dramatica gave my stories better structure. And sure, the software suggested possibilities I hadn't thought of for my script. And—I had to admit—my screenplays showed an overall improvement the more I grasped this theory. But...

Would that be enough to overcome the colossal truths of the trade, to defeat the market's hurdles and make a sale?

Just to get past my insecurity, I resolved to put aside my doubts and keep learning, writing, and sending out my Dramatica-informed scripts.

And, lo and behold, one of those scripts got a positive answer from a producer. She asked me for a pitch meeting! She gave me the usual third degree about my story's structure, characters' personalities, use of genre, and thematic premise. But because I'd written this story with Dramatica, I could answer every question with precise, confident answers. At the end of the session, the producer had nothing else to ask, and the story structure still stood as pristine as the Pellegrino water on her desk. She gave me a curious look—which became a warm smile as she said:

"Well, you obviously know what you're doing."

Of course she asked me for a rewrite—but for the very first time in my life, a producer spent a whole hour of her busy schedule giving me enthusiastic suggestions about how I should do the rewrite!

I went home to work on the rewrite with a newfound self-confidence. My credibility was greatly enhanced when I used my *Dramatica* learning to explain the story's structure. I had a hunch that, because of Dramatica, I had shown this producer a level of knowledge and expertise she'd rarely seen—and thus I'd finally taken the first step toward "the other side of the market."

More importantly, the rewrite came out *exactly* as the producer wanted it. Since I wrote it with software that gave me complete control over the plot, characters, theme and story ending, this was a cinch. She congratulated me and asked me to participate on several newer, bigger, more important projects.

From then on, my life as a writer changed. I was on the "A-list." I got a couple of large projects to develop. Some big-shot producers started asking me for opinions on their optioned screenplays. The Berlin Festival level directors gave me their personal phone numbers. I gave a couple of lectures on story analysis, and got a regular gig teaching a class for screenwriters. My students were happy. The producers were happy. I was happy.

The best part was, the things I wrote were no longer competing in that 40,000-script race. I'd earned the right to actually be read, instead of just being thrown into the pile. The big shots had started viewing me as an "up-and-coming writer," instead of an "unknown wanna-be." I was getting through to producers instead of just their personal assistants. The market was considering me, not automatically dismissing me, all because I showed a producer that I knew what I was doing—once.

> **DRAMATICA DOESN'T GUARANTEE THE SALE OF MY SCREENPLAY, BUT IT SURE HELPS ME SELL MYSELF AS A SCREENWRITER.**

Can it do the same for you?
I don't see why not.
But you'll have to pay the price. You'll have to master Dramatica.

Which leads us to the remaining question:

"Should I accept and abide by all of Dramatica's rules?"

I agonized over this…until I accepted:

"No, not really."

Not really, because Dramatica doesn't give me any "rules." It gives me a framework, a model to which I compare my story—to see where I want to follow the model closely, and where I want my story to fly free on its own. Dramatica is a set of writing tools:

- A compass that I can use to find navigational points whenever I lose my writing direction.

- A blueprint I can employ to disassemble a story and rebuild it.

- A grid I can use "behind my story," like a painter uses a grid to sketch in her initial composition lines before applying one dab of paint.

It turns out that Dramatica is NOT:

- The slate of commandments I initially thought it was.

- The implacable and cold Development Exec who throws formulas and arbitrary demands into my story.

- The shamanistic Writing-Theory-Of-The-Day that twists all scripts into its precepts.

> **DRAMATICA CONSISTS OF TOOLS TO DRAW UPON WHEN NEEDED AND LAY ASIDE WHEN NOT.**

And every time I work with it, I confirm that the Dramatica model is anything but arbitrary. It's a model where every story point (every plot event, every character trait, every thematic argument) supports all the other story points.

2

DRAMATICA'S ADVANTAGES

Before starting a project with Dramatica, you should know what to expect. As with any creative approach, Dramatica has its own special style, particular limits, and unique powers. Dramatica makes many writing tasks easier to accomplish. Others are still tricky, even with Dramatica. So you'd better know what you're going to get up front to help you decide when to go with Dramatica.

Here are some distinctive advantages of writing a story with Dramatica:

- **Dramatica Can Get You To Write Really Fast**

  You can finish a complete first draft in three months. Rewrite periods are even faster.

- **Dramatica Can Get You To Consider Ideas You Hadn't Thought Of.**

  It gives you perspectives on your story you hadn't contemplated – but producers or the audience will. With Dramatica's help, you'll arrive at a more complete, audience satisfying story.

- **Dramatica Allows You To Start Writing Your Story At Any Point While Assuring Perfect Sense**

  No more "don't type a letter until you have a solid premise" or "leave the dialogue for last." If you have a favorite scene and you can find a way to squeeze it into the storyform, the software will make sure the rest of your story fits in nicely, coherently, and entertainingly around it.

- **Dramatica Clarifies A Process That's Usually Trial and Error**

  With a little practice, you can accurately anticipate how any new idea would affect the whole story – which aspects fit and which don't— without even opening the software. Practice pays off.

- **A Dramatica Story Has "Heart"**

  The Dramatica model is structured in a way that won't allow you to
  ignore the inner workings of your characters. It will urge you to show
  their true nature and, at some point, make a significant change in
  a character's nature. As a result, your story compels your audience
  to identify with your characters and feel *moved*. A deep emotional
  response is the result of stories with *heart*.

- **A Dramatica Story Has Diversity**

  In the Dramatica model, every subject should grow until it reaches its
  last consequence. A story that starts with a simple problem develops
  into unsuspected predicaments and serious difficulties that stem from
  the original problem. Dramatica won't let you linger forever on the
  same issue.

- **A Dramatica Story Is Fully Developed**

  This means that every view, thread, and layer of your story is developed
  to its full potential and its ultimate stages. Dramatica separates your
  story into co-functional threads and components, makes you develop
  each one as an independent piece, then helps you rejoin them
  cohesively.

  This gives you a coherent theme and a plot without holes. But more
  importantly, it makes a convincing argument to the audience, a story
  that exhausts every alternative and independently considers every side
  before reaching its final, unavoidable conclusion.

There you have it. Dramatica may not be for everyone, but it is a great writing
tool if you learn how to use it.

Have you made your decision to continue reading? Then open your Dramatica
software and let's get into some actual writing.

SECTION II
THE OVERALL PICTURE

THE DIFFICULT DECISIONS OF STORYFORMING

3

STORYFORMING FROM A PREMISE

To create a complete story, to produce a cinematic masterpiece, many of us—simple, mortal screenwriters—start with a thematic *Premise* such as this one:

> *"Unconditional sacrifice leads to freedom."*

Okay, sounds typical.

But what is a premise?

A premise is a single sentence that holds the thematic core of the story. A premise is neither a universal truth nor a product of pristine logic. It's just a writing tool. It helps us in explaining our point to producers and co-writers, works wonders for shaping our drafts, and in the end, reflects our personal truth—the personal statement that will be fully demonstrated by the end of our movie.

Okay. Now, how do we get our premise?

A premise is made up of three parts that blend together, forming a coherent sentence. The intricate mix makes those parts a bit tricky to identify, but a little practice makes each piece of the premise clear.

The ingredients of a premise are:

- *Character*: The part of the premise that describes the nature or condition of a central individual in our story, such as *"merciful"* or *"impoverished."*

- *Plot*: The part of the premise that shows a major incident—or series of incidents—of our story, such as *"a violent death"* or *"innumerable quarrels."*

- *Theme*: The part of the premise that reveals the central area of discussion of the story, such as *"corruption by power"* or *"the existence of God."*

Easy, huh?

Well, the real trick is to identify which part is which. Look at the following premise:

"Insatiable ambition leads to self-destruction."

Which is the character part, which is the plot part, and which is the thematic part?

The sentence-mix makes each one blurry—the character part could seem the thematic part, and this can be confused with the plot. So, to answer this, we first have to break the premise into three parts:

- *Insatiable*

- *Ambition*

- *Leads to self-destruction.*

Now to identify which is which:

- *"Insatiable"*: This is a moral condition, a human nature; it describes a person who's always wanting. Let's make this is the character part of the premise.

- *"Ambition"*: What is ambition? Every human has his own definition of it. It can be morally shameful or an essential trait to survive. A controversial topic, we'll make "ambition" the thematic part of the premise.

- *"Leads to self-destruction"*: This suggests the final incident, the final change of the story. This is our plot part of the premise.

So, "Insatiable ambition leads to self-destruction" is a premise comprised of character (*insatiable*), theme (*ambition*), and plot (*leads to self-destruction*).

This one was easy enough. Let's look at a trickier example:

"Excessive thinking leads to painful realizations."

Now, for a little premise analysis:

- *"Excessive"*: How can we tell when someone is being excessive? That which may be excessive at a royal banquet may be acceptable at a football game. We can't tell if someone is being "excessive" without an incident or context that makes us appraise it. This is going to be our plot part of the premise.

- *"**Thinking**"*: This is an action, a task of the human brain. Someone has to do the thinking. Let's make this the character part of the premise.

- *"**Leads to painful realizations**"*: How painful is painful? Is pain bad? What is worse—to know the hurtful truth or to live in a blissful lie? This will be our theme. No questions here.

So, *"Excessive thinking leads to painful realizations"* is a premise that blends plot (*excessive*), character (*thinking*), and theme (*leads to painful realizations*).

Premise analysis is not a piece of cake. A story analyst needs to read the whole script to understand and break down the premise. For a writer, it is better to first write some story sketches and then ask ourselves, "How can I define my character?" "Which is a major event in my plot?" "What is my theme?" Ask yourself questions to extract succinct concepts and form a premise from those.

Let's do one more example before applying all this to Dramatica:

"Unconditional sacrifice leads to freedom."

Break it down:

- *"**Unconditional**"*: What's "unconditional"? Can something have no strings attached whatever? Can "unconditional" mask a selfish purpose? An item for discussion, this is our theme.

- *"**Sacrifice**"*: At some point in the story someone must die or endure a significant loss—a plot event.

- *"**Leads to freedom**"*: To be freed, someone had to be enslaved or imprisoned in some way. This is our character condition.

Okay, so, *"unconditional sacrifice leads to freedom"* is a premise made of theme, plot, and character.

Now...

How does this all fit in Dramatica? Let's launch our software to find out.

Open the *Story Engine* screen. We find everything we need to turn our premise into the beginning of a storyform in Dramatica's Story Engine.

Here's how we storyform from a premise:

- The *character* part of the premise tells us how to storyform the *Main Character Dynamics* and the *Main Character Story Points*.

- The *plot* part of the premise tells us how to storyform the *OS Plot Dynamics* and the *Additional OS Story Points*.

- The *Theme* part of the premise tells us how to storyform the *OS Themes*.

Let's take our premises for a test drive:

"Insatiable ambition leads to self-destruction."

- *"Insatiable"* as a *Main Character Dynamic* means the *Main Character's Growth should Stop*, because his hunger makes him unquenchable. Regarding the Main Character, the audience is waiting for something to end.

- *"Ambition"* as an *OS Theme* suggests an *OS Issue of Self-Interest*, since that fits with a strong drive for success. Based on our choice of OS Issue, thematic focus of the Overall Story is doing or being based on what is best for oneself.

- *"Leads to self-destruction"* as a *Plot Dynamic* stands for a *Judgment of Bad results*, since it is a subtle but satisfactory description of "self-destruction." The outcome of the Main Character's efforts fail in resolving his personal problems.

To storyform from a premise we need to break down our premise first and clearly identify the *character* part, the *plot* part, and the *theme* part. Then, match each part to specific Story Engine sections and, finally, translate our premise concepts into Dramatica story points.

Kind of like storyencoding (illustrating story points) in reverse.

Let's do another exercise:

"Excessive thinking leads to painful realizations."

- *"Excessive"*—Remember we needed an event to show this one? Let's choose an *OS Plot Dynamic Limit of Optionlock*. This way we can pinpoint when the excessive behavior breaks the limit. The story climax occurs because all options have been exhausted.

- *"Thinking"* as a *Main Character Dynamic* suggests an *Approach* of *Be-er*, which gives us an immersed, meditative character. The Main Character prefers to work things out internally.

- *"Leads to Painful Realizations"* as an *OS Theme* suggests an *Issue* of *Truth*, and we can make that truth as painful as we need it. The Overall Story's thematic focus is about that which is actually correct or factual.

Now, if you're checking all these story points with the software, you'll see that each choice draws you closer to a complete storyform but not all the way.

Storyforming from a premise leaves us with more than a hundred storyforms from which to find the single storyform that best describes our story. That's the nature of the premise. It's just a beginning, a point of departure from where our story can take off and develop.

We should keep in mind that, in the end, most stories have no strict resemblance to the premise that produced them. A premise is just a tool to get us started, not the final word on how we should write our screenplay.

Let's do one more:

> *"Unconditional sacrifice leads to freedom."*

- *"Unconditional"* as an *OS Theme* suggests an *OS Issue of Morality,* and that gives us a broad area for our thematic discussion. The story's thematic focus is about doing or being based on what is best for others.

- *"Sacrifice"* as an *OS Plot Dynamic* represents a *Driver of Action*, and the "sacrifice" is a major event in our plot. In our story, actions force decisions.

- *"Leads to freedom"* as a *Main Character Dynamic* stands for a *Main Character's Growth of Stop*. In this case, this equates to stopping the imprisonment. Regarding the Main Character, the audience is waiting for something to end.

Important: keep in mind that premise analysis and creation are not exact sciences. A piece of a premise that clearly seems like a character part to one author, may look like an obvious theme part to another. Also, an undeniable Dramatica choice for one screenwriter may seem completely wrong for another.

Again, a premise is a writing tool. It is only useful if it helps our writing.

4

DRAMATICA IN THIRTY SECONDS

Not actually thirty seconds—more like ten minutes—but anyway, this is a fast and fun method to evaluate if a storyform fits, to fine-tune a storyform, and to create a solid brief synopsis to start our storytelling.

Cool, huh? Here it is in a nutshell:

- *Driver + Consequence*

- *Goal + Requirements*

- *Forewarnings + Limit*

- *Driver + Outcome*

Here's how it works:

Example 1: A Horror Story

Suppose we're writing a ***Horror Story*** about a haunted house, and we have set our storyform to the following items:

> *Driver:* **Decision**
>
> *Limit:* **Timelock**
>
> *Outcome:* **Success**
>
> *Goal:* **The Future**
>
> *Consequence:* **Innermost Desires**
>
> *Requirements:* **The Present**
>
> *Forewarnings:* **Gathering Information**

First we start by putting these items in the following order:

- Decision *(Driver)* + Innermost Desires *(Consequence)*

- The Future *(Goal)* + The Present *(Requirements)*

- Learning *(Forewarnings)* + Timelock *(Limit)*

- Decision *(Driver)* + Success *(Outcome)*

Now we write a short synopsis consisting of four short paragraphs:

- The *1ˢᵗ Paragraph* tells the beginning of our story by blending the *Driver* and the story's *Consequence*.

- The *2ⁿᵈ Paragraph* recounts our story's development by blending the *Goal* and the *Requirements*.

- The *3ʳᵈ Paragraph* describes the critical moment that forces the characters to a decision (that is the Crisis) by blending the *Forewarnings* and the *Limit*.

- And the *4ᵗʰ Paragraph* tells how the story ends by blending another instance of the *Driver* and the *Outcome*.

We end up with something like this:

> "To change her shy personality and stop her subconscious fears *(Consequence* of *Innermost Desires)*, a teenager decides to join her friends for a party at an allegedly haunted house *(Driver* of *Decision)*."

> "Unexplainable events start killing the group of teenagers one by one. They must survive this terrifying current situation *(Requirements* of *The Present)* and escape to secure their future *(Goal* of *The Future)*."

> "The few survivors wait until sunrise—when the house's curse is supposed to end *(Timelock Limit),* but a few minutes before dawn, they find a clue that one of them is the murderer *(Forewarnings* of *Learning)*. Unmasked, he tries to kill them all."

> "The shy girl decides to face the killer *(Driver* of *Decision)* and gets him to fall into one of his own traps, saving herself and the remaining teenagers *(Outcome* of *Success)*."

That's it, neat and simple. It's enough to give us a clear idea of our storyform, to evaluate if it's the way we want it to go, and if so, to start telling our screenplay.

If not, this is the time to choose:

- If our story needs an *Action Driver* instead of a *Decision Driver*.

- If our *Consequence* should be *The Past* instead of *Innermost Desires*.

- Or, if our *Goal* should be *Developing a Plan* instead of *The Future*.

With our four-paragraph synopsis, structure changes come easily. Better to do them now than when we are on page 117 of our final draft.

Example 2: A Courtroom Drama

Let's do another example: A ***Courtroom Drama*** about a woman unjustly accused of murder.

Here are the storyform Items:

- Action *(Driver)* + The Present *(Consequence)*

- Contemplation *(Goal)* + Innermost Desires *(Requirements)*

- Changing One's Nature *(Forewarnings)* + Optionlock *(Limit)*

- Action *(Driver)* + Failure *(Outcome)*.

Let's give it a try and write our four paragraphs:

- "A married man is discovered dead *(Driver* of *Action)*, and evidence incriminates his lover, so she is arrested and put in jail during the trial *(Consequence* of *The Present)*."

- "Her lawyer presents several arguments that should make the jurors consider her innocence *(Goal* of *Contemplation)*, but she's an adulterer which drives the jurors' emotions against her *(Requirements* of *Innermost Desires)*."

- "This harrowing experience changes her and makes her tough *(Forewarnings* of *Changing One's Nature)*. The sexual implications of the charges bring her unbearable sexual harassment by the bailiffs and prison guards, until she can't stand it any longer *(Limit* of *Optionlock)*."

- "This situation takes her to a point where she attacks a bailiff *(Driver* of *Action)*, and this act condemns her in the jurors' eyes. She is declared guilty and sentenced to death *(Outcome* of *Failure)*."

That's okay for a first draft—though it could improve if we upgrade the storytelling a little:

> *"Sarah is a shy woman who falls for a married man. Even though she's against adultery, she starts an affair with him. One day, her lover tells Sarah they should end their affair. She agrees, and they say farewell amicably. The next day he is found dead in the same hotel room where they used to meet. The hotel clerk identifies Sarah as the last person who saw him. Sarah is arrested. Word hits the media, and suddenly Sarah becomes the "adulteress-murderer" in all the tabloids. Sarah's lawyers present hard evidence of her innocence, but the jury is biased because of her adulterous behavior and is not convinced. While imprisoned, Sarah is also under the constant sexual harassment of a sinister bailiff. The media pressure, the prosecution, and the officer's harassment are too much for Sarah who assaults the menacing bailiff right in the courtroom. This is seen by the jury as the clear evidence of Sarah's guilt. She's pronounced guilty and sentenced to death."*

There, with the same storyform items, we now have a synopsis strong enough for a pitch meeting.

Still, this is only a partial view of our story. Just some of the major events to see if we—and the producers—like this particular storyform or another. From here we develop our story. We have the rest of this book to do so.

Example 3: An Action/Historical Drama

But, for now, let's do another example: How about an ***Action/Historical Drama*** about the Hindenburg Disaster?

Here are our items:

- Decision *(Driver)* + Changing One's Nature *(Consequence)*

- Obtaining *(Goal)* + Doing *(Requirements)*

- Impulsive Responses *(Forewarnings)* + Optionlock *(Limit)*

- Decision *(Driver)* + Failure *(Outcome)*

Now let's do it:

- "To avoid being transformed by the rabid Nazi ideology *(Consequence* of *Changing One's Nature)*, a young German decides to flee his country *(Driver* of *Decision)* by getting a job on the Hindenburg and a passage to America."

- "His idea is to escape on arrival at Lakehurst, to ask for political protection, and eventually to gain American citizenship *(Goal* of *Obtaining).* His plan is jeopardized because he enrolled and served in the Nazi Party *(Requirements* of *Doing)* to get the job on the zeppelin."

- "Onboard the aircraft the young man feels impulsively attracted to an American woman *(Forewarnings* of *Impulsive Responses)* who is presumed to be of Jewish descent. A Nazi Officer notices and puts the young man under veiled observation until the young man has no choice but to confess he doesn't believe in the Nazi ideology *(Limit* of *Optionlock)."*

- "At the moment of the fire, the Nazi Official offers the young man a quick exit—with a tacit debt to the Nazi Party—but the young man refuses and stays aboard to help the American woman *(Driver* of *Decision).* He saves her, still happy that he's made the right decision, but loses his life *(Outcome* of *Failure)."*

Try writing several drafts of your synopsis, experimenting with different storyforms, exploring the possibilities, and going crazy. Try everything until you find the storyform that truly fits the story you want to write.

Now, with a synopsis based on structure, a strong premise, clearly defined characters, and a setting based on our genre, it will be a breeze to complete the perfect storyform for our story and write the treatment from it.

5

NEW INSTANT DRAMATICA

Through the years I've used this technique called "Instant Dramatica" to write everything from step outlines, to treatments, to basic first drafts. With every written script, this method develops a little and gets easier, faster, more complete and more comprehensive. In its latest form, "Instant Dramatica" quickly gives me a step outline of forty or more events from which I can write a treatment or a rudimentary script.

Here it is, the *"New Instant Dramatica."*

To start we need three things: A good initial idea, a solid premise, and a clearly defined genre. For this example let's make a ***Romantic Comedy*** (*genre*) about "A guy who falls in love with a girl passing by on a bus" (*initial idea*), and proves that "Impulsive love leads to happiness" (*premise*).

We begin working on our storyform by choosing our genre (Appendix C, *Genre and the Dramatica Domains*). A ***Romantic Comedy*** usually has an Subjective Story Domain of Activities. That gives us an Overall Story Domain of Manipulation. Let's mark it.

Then we continue it by analyzing our premise (chapter three, *Storyforming from a Premise*). "Impulsive love leads to happiness" analyzed in terms of "Impulsive." An impulsive action drives the story and gives us a *Plot Driver* of *Action*. "Love" suggests our thematic matter is about emotions, and this gives us an *Overall Story Issue of Circumstances*—an emotional assessment of the environment. "Leads to happiness" means the character starts being happy, so this is a *Character Growth* of *Start*. Let's select these entries.

Now we can choose some more items to complete our storyform. Based on our instincts, we make these additional story choices: *Resolve* = Change; *Approach* = Do-er; *Mental Sex* = Male; *Limit* = Optionlock; *Outcome* = Success; *Judgment* = Good; *OS Problem* = Aware.

Brief Synopsis

What is important is that we can check out the items we've chosen and the entire storyform with a *Brief Synopsis* (chapter four, *Dramatica In Thirty Seconds*) like this one:

- "At 35, Alex thought he knew everything about love and believed 'love at first sight' was a myth *(Consequence* of *Understanding).* That's what he thought until the day he saw that beautiful woman passing by on a bus and fell immediately in love with her *(Initial Driver* of *Action)."*

- "Now Alex spends his days thinking of far-fetched plans to find that woman and seduce her *(Goal* of *Developing a Plan),* but he doesn't even know who she is. He imagines her as a hallucination, a dream-woman beyond reach *(Requirements* of *Conceiving an Idea)."*

- "Meanwhile, Alex is engaged to a woman he doesn't love *(Forewarnings* of *The Present).* His fiancée feels him drift away and urges him to choose between his dreams of love and her *(Limit* of *Optionlock).* Alex opts for his fiancée and makes a vow to forget the woman on the bus."

- "The day of the wedding, Alex sees that woman on the bus again and leaves the ceremony to go after her *(Final Driver* of *Action).* He finally meets her and finds true love *(Outcome* of *Success)."*

Create Characters

From our synopsis some characters are starting to emerge. Alex is one of them, and so is the Girl On The Bus. Alex's fiancée is the other one. The time has come to create some characters for our story and to start thinking of traits and behaviors for them. The following chapters in this book will help you.

Creating characters at this point is fun and productive as long as we realize that none of our decisions are etched in stone. Further along, characters that seemed central may turn superfluous, and we should delete them mercilessly. We may also create new characters as the story needs them.

One critical decision should be made at this point and should remain consistent throughout our story development. We should identify our Main and Impact Characters. For this **Romantic Comedy**, the lovers should be the Main Character and Impact Character—but in this story the couple doesn't get together until the end. Is it be possible to write a love story like this? Let's find out.

Find a "Title" for Each Throughline

This is the moment to learn what our throughlines are all about. Here's the "Instant Dramatica" way to do it. Mixing the *Domain, Concern,* and *Problem* of each *Throughline* we can find a title for that particular throughline that later makes creating material for it effortless.

Let's see:

- The Overall Story has a *Manipulation Domain,* a *Developing a Plan Concern,* and an *Aware Problem.* This means that all the characters *(Overall Story)* have twisted ways of thinking *(Manipulation Domain)* and develop complicated plans *(Developing a Plan Concern)* because they're too aware of things outside themselves *(Aware Problem).* Now, what do you call a story about these wacky characters that plan and over-prepare for outward appearance? How about *"Strategy For Status"* or *"Aristocratic Neurotics"*? Any title that reminds you of the description above is fine.

- The Main Character is in an awkward situation *(Situation Domain)* caused by what has already happened to him *(The Past Concern),* and it makes him excessively aware of things outside himself *(Aware Problem).* This could be a story about a guy who got engaged too soon because of previous heartbreaks and is oversensitive to rejection. *"Unlucky In Love"* is a good title.

- The Impact Character forms fixed attitudes *(Fixed Attitude Domain)* caused by odd recollections *(Memory Concern)* and tends to see dire events in the future *(Projection Problem).* We can make this a story about a Girl who always gets involved in ugly obsessive affairs, because she somehow reminds men of long-lost loves. Therefore, she avoids any relationship because they all will end in disaster. Let's title this, *"Wrong Dream Girl."*

- The Main and Impact Characters (Subjective Story) engage in a series of activities *(Activities Domain)* because they don't grasp *(Understanding Concern)* how things are organized *(Order Problem).* Alex and the Girl On The Bus will try to find each other, but their searching will get so frenetic and their 'sign-reading' so mistaken that they'll miss each other every time. *"Mutual Misplacements"* is this throughline's title.

Now we know what our throughlines are all about—and yes, writing this romance where the lovers are unable to find each other seems possible—but how does this all come together? Let's look at the core of our story to find out.

Create A Synopsis For The Character Arc

To illustrate the emotional heart of our story, we're going to create another four-paragraph synopsis:

- The *1ˢᵗ Paragraph* portrays the beginning of the story by combining the *Main Character's Crucial Element* and the *Impact Character's Crucial Element* (look at the "Build Characters" screen in the Dramatica® Pro software for them).

- The *2ⁿᵈ Paragraph* relates the story development by describing solely the *Main Character's Growth*.

- The *3ʳᵈ Paragraph* tells the story Crisis by blending the *Main Character's Resolve* and the *Impact Character's Resolve*.

- The *4ᵗʰ Paragraph* says how the story ends with the *Main Character's Judgment*.

Let's see:

- "Alex puts on a facade of happiness and fulfillment with his new engagement *(Main Character's Crucial Element* of *Aware)*. When he meets the Girl On The Bus, he realizes something's missing in his love life *(Impact Character's Crucial Element* of *Self-Aware).*"

- "So Alex starts looking for that someone to fill the hole in his heart *(Main Character's Growth* of *Start).*"

- "Alex finds his inner needs *(Main Character's Resolve* of *Change)* by searching for that enigmatic Girl On The Bus *(Impact Character's Resolve* of *Steadfast).*"

- "Alex is happy and fulfilled in the end *(Main Character's Judgment* of *Good).*"

Good **Romantic Comedy** stuff.

Create Summaries of Each Throughline

Now we're ready to develop the rest of our story, and we're going to do it with four paragraph synopses. First, we need summaries of each throughline's story points. Here's how to do it:

- The *1ˢᵗ Paragraph* of each synopsis tells the beginning of the story by combining a Throughline's *Domain* and *Concern*.

- The *2nd Paragraph* describes the story's development by blending the Throughline's *Issue* and *Counterpoint*.

- The *3rd Paragraph* shows the Crisis by using the Throughline's *Symptom* and *Response*.

- And the *4th Paragraph* reveals the end with the Throughline's *Problem* and *Solution*.

Overall Story Throughline Summary

Let's start with the Overall Story throughline. This will be a breeze with all the work we did in finding a title for our Throughlines. Here it goes:

Overall Story: "Aristocratic Neurotics"

- "The characters are mostly upper-class neurotics *(Overall Story Domain of Manipulation)* who meticulously prepare for any insignificant event *(Overall Story Concern of Developing a Plan)*."

- "In their thirties, the characters feel lonely *(Overall Story Issue of Circumstances)* and rush into empty relationships, dismissing true love as nonexistent *(Overall Story Counterpoint of Situation)*."

- "These empty relationships make them feel cheated by life *(Overall Story Symptom of Inequity),* and they start compensating for it by acting like 'filthy rich' jerks and rejecting anyone who has less than they do *(Overall Story Response of Equity)*."

- "They realize their unhappiness is caused by their attention to status and external appearances *(Overall Story Problem of Aware)* and start looking into themselves to find their true emotions *(Overall Story Solution of Self-Aware)*."

There, that should give us a broad idea of our Overall Story. With this broad idea in mind, we'll follow by telling the throughline's plot development. We're going to use the Overall Story Signposts. To make this procedure painless, we'll start by writing a paragraph that describes how each Signpost follows the others. We'll start with the Signposts:

- *OS Signpost # 1:* Developing A Plan *(Conceptualizing)*

- *OS Signpost # 2:* Conceiving An Idea *(Conceiving)*

- *OS Signpost # 3:* Playing A Role *(Being)*

- *OS Signpost # 4:* Changing One's Nature *(Becoming)*

And arrange them into a paragraph:

> *"They Make Plans, and those Plans lead them to Invent something,*
> *and those Inventions lead them to Pretend, and this Pretending leads*
> *them to Change Their Nature."*

Now we're ready to write yet another four paragraph synopsis of the Overall Story Plot Development with each Signpost as a paragraph:

- "The characters realize the plans they had for a happy love life have gone awry *(Developing A Plan)*."

- "The characters imagine 'true love' as pure illusion *(Conceiving an Idea)*."

- "The characters live according to their new philosophy—insincere love is better than the illusion of true love *(Playing a Role)*."

- "The characters change their nature to improve their love lives *(Changing One's Nature)*."

Main Character Throughline Summary

Now we have the basis of our Overall Story. We have a Four Paragraph Synopsis of its Story Points and another Four Paragraph Synopsis of its Plot Development. Let's do the same for the other three throughlines. Shall we?

Main Character Story: "Unlucky In Love"

- "Because of past bitter lost loves *(Main Character Concern* of *The Past)*, Alex proposes to a woman he doesn't love. Before he knows it, his situation changes from the bachelor life to a fiancé's existence *(Main Character Domain* of *Situation)*."

- "Alex persuades himself to accept his future marriage *(Main Character Issue* of *Destiny)*, but keeps postponing the wedding day and avoids his fiancée's attempts to move into his apartment *(Main Character Counterpoint* of *Fate)*."

- "Deep inside, Alex hopes that suddenly he will start loving his fiancée *(Main Character Symptom* of *Speculation)*. Even deeper inside he knows this relationship will end in heartbreak—like all his others *(Main Character Response* of *Projection)*. He is constantly tempted to break off this phony engagement."

- "But Alex doesn't break the engagement for fear of hurting his fiancée's feelings *(Main Character Problem of Aware)*, though he's miserable, until he starts examining his own feelings *(Main Character Solution* of *Self-Aware)*."

Now, let's do the *Main Character's Plot Synopsis* and start with the signposts assembling sentence:

"Alex's life Progresses, and this Progress alters his Future, and this new Future alters his Present, and this new Present alters his Past."

Now, the Synopsis:

- "Alex's life changes radically the moment he gets engaged *(Main Character Signpost # 1: Progress—i.e. how things are changing)*."

- "Alex shows signs of extreme apprehension when confronted with his future as a married man *(Main Character Signpost # 2: Future)*."

- "The wedding day is here and now *(Main Character Signpost # 3: Present)*. Alex's loveless marriage seems certain."

- "Alex finds the Girl On The Bus and finally has a possibility to break the endless line of heartbreaks of his past *(Main Character Signpost # 4: Past)*."

Impact Character Throughline Summary

Now let's work on the Impact Character Story:

Impact Character Story: "Wrong Dream Girl"

- "The Girl On The Bus has a history of obsessive love relationships *(Impact Character Domain Fixed Attitude)* where all her boyfriends find her eerily like former lost loves *(Impact Character Concern Memory)*."

- "She feels compelled to break these relationships based on false 'fixations' *(Impact Character Issue* of *Falsehood)*, and thus, this beautiful woman always ends up alone, unable to find true love *(Impact Character Counterpoint* of *Truth)*."

- "She feels it's her fault in creating those obsessions and thinks she's being unfair to her boyfriends *(Impact Character Symptom* of *Inequity)*. Therefore she thinks it only fair she's alone *(Impact Character Response* of *Equity)*."

- "She likes to think of the possibility that somewhere there's a man who will love her for who she really is *(Impact Character Solution of Speculation)* but, since none of her relationships has worked so far *(Impact Character Problem of Projection)*, she avoids all relationships."

Now the IC's Plot Development:

"The Girl On The Bus creates Memories. Those Memories create Reactions (Impulsive Responses). Those Reactions create Emotions (Innermost Desires), and those Emotions create new Considerations (Contemplation)"

- "The Girl On The Bus watches Alex through the bus window, and for the first time in her life, she experiences what many men have experienced with her. Alex reminds her of a long-lost love *(Impact Character Signpost # 1 Memory)*."

- "The Girl On The Bus starts seeing Alex's face everywhere, but the images are only hallucinations *(Impact Character Signpost # 2 Impulsive Responses)*."

- "The Girl On The Bus realizes she has fallen in love with a guy she hasn't met yet *(Impact Character Signpost # 3 Innermost Desires)*."

- "The Girl On The Bus meets Alex but considers that she will break his heart like she does with all her boyfriends. She thinks of ways to get away from him *(Impact Character Signpost # 4 Contemplation)*."

Subjective Story Throughline Summary

Okay, finally let's write our Main vs. Impact (Subjective) Story:

Subjective Story: "Mutual Misplacements"

- "Alex looks for the Girl On The Bus while she unconsciously searches for him *(Subjective Story Domain Activities)*, but they misunderstand all the signs *(Subjective Story Concern Understanding)*, and mutually look for each other in all the wrong places."

- "They think this fruitless search means that their love is not meant to be *(Subjective Story Issue of Interpretation)*. Whenever they give up, they see each other far away *(Subjective Story Counterpoint of Senses)*—too late to make contact—but with enough certainty to try to find each other again."

- "Alex is obviously of an upper class, while The Girl On The Bus is a working woman. They think this difference—and their different environments—is the main cause they can't find each other *(Subjective Story Symptom* of *Inequity)*. So, they try to fathom how and where 'the other half lives' to find each other *(Subjective Story Response* of *Equity)*."

- "The mutual search is unsuccessful, because it is too restricted and limited *(Subjective Story Problem* of *Order)*. It is not until they let things happen that they bump fortuitously into each other again *(Subjective Story Solution* of *Chaos)*."

Fine. And the Plot Development:

> *"Alex and the Girl On The Bus Understand something. That Understanding leads them to Do something. This Doing leads them to Learn something. This Learning finally lets them Obtain something."*

- "Alex and The Girl On The Bus understand they won't be able to rest until they find each other *(Subjective Story Signpost # 1 Understanding)*."

- "Alex and The Girl On The Bus search frenetically for each other *(Subjective Story Signpost # 2 Doing)*."

- "The Girl On The Bus tries to gather information about whom Alex is, while he does the same for her *(Subjective Story Signpost # 3 Learning)*."

- "Alex and The Girl On The Bus finally get together *(Subjective Story Signpost # 4 Obtaining)*."

There, we've done enough writing for the day.

Synopses Recap

As you can see, we've created ten Four-Paragraph Synopses:

- **The Plot Synopsis:** Consists of Initial Driver, Consequence, Goal, Requirements, Limit, Forewarnings, Final Driver and Outcome.

- **The Character Arc Synopsis:** Main Character's Crucial Element, Impact Character's Crucial Element, Main Character's Growth, Main Character's Resolve, Impact Character's Resolve, and Main Character's Judgment.

- **The Overall Story Synopsis:** OS Domain, OS Concern, OS Issue, OS Counterpoint, OS Symptom, OS Response, OS Problem, and OS Solution.

- **The Overall Story Development Synopsis:** The four OS Signposts.

- **The Main Character's Synopsis:** MC Domain, MC Concern, MC Issue, MC Counterpoint, MC Symptom, MC Response, MC Problem, and MC Solution.

- **The Main Character's Development Synopsis:** All four MC Signposts.

- **The Impact Character Synopsis:** IC Domain, IC Concern, IC Issue, IC Counterpoint, IC Symptom, IC Response, IC Problem, and IC Solution.

- **The Impact Character Development Synopsis:** The four IC Signposts.

- **The Subjective Story Synopsis**: SS Domain, SS Concern, SS Issue, SS Counterpoint, SS Symptom, SS Response, SS Problem, and SS Solution.

- **The Subjective Story Development Synopsis**: The four SS Signposts.

Create A Forty-Scene Step Outline

What shall we do now with all these synopses? How can we make these paragraphs tell our story?

Well, we'll order our paragraphs to create a forty-scene step outline. That's how.

Here are the "rules of thumb":

- The *1ˢᵗ Paragraph* of each *Synopsis* goes into *Act I* of our Step Outline.

- The *2ⁿᵈ Paragraphs* of the *Synopses* go into the *First Half of Act II*.

- The *3ʳᵈ Paragraphs* go into the *Second Half of Act II*.

- The *4ᵗʰ Paragraphs* go into *Act III*.

The idea is to arrange the Paragraphs within each Act—or half-Act in Act II—in an order that has dramatic flow, to sort them in a way they tell the story you want to tell.

Here's an example of how the first ten of the forty scenes in the step outline might appear in our sample story:

"Act I:

- "The characters are mostly neurotics of an upper-class level and meticulously prepare for any insignificant event *(OS Domain* and *Concern* from the *OS Synopsis)*."

- "The characters realize the plans they had for a happy love life have gone awry *(OS Signpost # 1)*."

- "Because of past bitter lost loves, Alex proposes to a woman he doesn't love, and before he knows it, his situation changes from the bachelor life to a fiancé's existence *(MC Concern* and *Domain* from the *MC Synopsis)*."

- "Alex's life changes radically the moment he gets engaged *(MC Signpost # 1)*."

- "At 35, Alex thought he knew everything about love and believed 'love at first sight' was a myth. That is, until the day he saw that beautiful woman passing by on a bus and fell immediately in love with her *(Consequence* and *Initial Driver* from the *Plot Synopsis)*."

- "The Girl On The Bus watches Alex through the bus window, and for the first time in her life, she experiences what many men have experienced with her. Alex reminds her of a long-lost love *(IC Signpost # 1)*."

- "The Girl On The Bus has a history of obsessive love relationships where all her boyfriends find her eerily similar to former lost loves *(IC Domain* and *Concern* from the *IC Synopsis)*."

- "Alex puts on a facade of happiness and fulfillment with his new engagement, but when he meets the Girl On The Bus, he realizes something's missing in his love life *(Main and Impact Characters' Crucial Elements* from the *Character-Arc Synopsis)*."

- "Alex and the Girl On The Bus understand they won't be able to rest until they find each other *(SS Signpost # 1)*."

- "Alex looks for the Girl On The Bus while she unconsciously searches for him, but they misunderstand all the signs and mutually look for each other in all the wrong places *(SS Domain* and *Concern* from the *SS Synopsis)*."

Turn The Step Outline Into A Treatment or Screenplay

From this step outline we can just change the phrasing to give it narrative drive or find concrete, dramatic illustrations for each paragraph and turn it into a treatment or even into a screenplay.

Say, *"The characters are mostly neurotics of an upper-class level and meticulously prepare for any insignificant event"* could be turned into:

```
EXT.  JEWELRY STORE - DAY

A classy and very expensive-looking
establishment.


INT.  JEWELRY STORE - DAY

ALEX and his friend HUGH stand in front of the
high-security glass counter, looking in turn
at two items inside the counter.  Anxiety shows
in their faces.  Alex takes a deep breath and
points at one item timidly.
```

                        ALEX
                 Okay, I think--

Hugh cuts him off.

                        HUGH
                 Wait. Alex, you're about
                 to choose your engagement
                 ring, probably the most
                 crucial decision in your
                 marriage. Have you given
                 it enough consideration?

                        ALEX
                 I—I think I'll take the one
                 on the left.

Hugh looks at it distastefully.

                        HUGH
                 The one on the left? Don't
                 you find it... uh, tedious,
                 dull?

Alex stops to think for a second and points at
the other item.

                        ALEX
                 Okay, then the one on the
                 right.

Hugh shrugs.

                        HUGH
                 The one on the right? Oh,
                 it's so not you.

Alex looks at him inquiringly.

                        HUGH
                 What can I say? You're a
                 tedious-dull kind of guy.

Alex stops to think for a second and points at
the first item.

                        ALEX
                 I'll take the one on the
                 left.

```
A CLERK approaches.

                    CLERK
              Fine choice, sir.

The clerk opens the counter, takes out a catalog
of engagement rings, puts it in a bag, and hands
it to Alex.

Hugh puts a hand on Alex's shoulder.

                    HUGH
              Now we just have to choose
              between two hundred rings,
              and you'll be on your way
              to marital bliss.

Alex sighs silently.
```

Instant Dramatica gives us a complete but rough structure of our story. It's the haziest grid we could draw to start to sketch our screenplay. Okay for a beginning, but surely we can take advantage of the many more defined profiles that Dramatica can give us.

For starters, let's see what Dramatica can do for our characters.

SECTION III
CHARACTERS

BEYOND THE ARCHETYPES

6

TRUE CHARACTER

Stop me if you've heard this one. A screenwriter takes her *Fantasy Saga* to a producer and weeks later he rejects it by saying, "There's one character, the Magic Elf, that can only be seen at twilight—the one with the big golden horns, the purple wings, the four sets of multicolored eyes, and the aurora borealis shining out of his belly..."

"What about him?"

"Well, he doesn't feel... real."

While it's true that producers sometimes make comments like that, it's also true that great authors can create characters as far-fetched as the elf above and yet make them feel as real as our closest buddies. It's as if we knew a person just like that elf and could talk to it. They're characters that immediately remind us of someone and compel us to tell that person, "You've got to see it; the elf is just like you!"

Creating such real characters has less to do with depicting our acquaintances in our story, or with studying real people and forcing their traits into our movie, than it does with *Consistency*.

In this context, consistency means *a character who acts and decides according to his own nature*, as opposed to a character who acts and decides according to whatever the plot tells him. For example, the violent biker who's suddenly scared of a teenage girl just because she happens to be the movie's hero, or the middle-aged, chubby accountant who unexpectedly leaps from rooftop to rooftop to escape from a killer. These inconsistent characters make the audience feel cheated and say, "This cannot happen in real life—no one can be like that."

Conversely, consistent characters with persistent desires, drives, limitations and principles are clear on what can be expected from them and let the viewers:

- *Develop a sense of reliability*—"See? I knew the accountant would never dare to try to jump."

- *Identify with them*—"That's what I'd do if I were him."

- *Get to know them as they know their buddies*—"Didn't I tell you he was gonna do that?"

When the audience knows what the character likes and dislikes, knows his habits, desires, drives, limitations, and principles, the character becomes real. However...

A consistent character shouldn't be without twists and complexity. The danger with consistent characters is that you may end up writing cardboard-cutout stereotypes who do one thing and one thing only. For example, the aggressive soldier who fears nothing and just lives to fight, or the seductive tempter who does nothing but solicit sex. These characters are consistent but also can be predictable and, well, plain boring.

Is there a way to write reliable yet interesting characters? Is it possible to have consistency and diversity at the same time?

Dramatica has "Build Character" screens to create such characters.

These screens are like maps of our characters' natures that allow us to put together the wildest personalities, yet make them consistent.

Questions To Ask About Your Characters

Before we launch our Dramatica software, we have to answer four questions about each of our characters:

- *What Does The Character Want?* What are his desires? What are his secret plans? What does he say when someone asks him what's he going to do with his life?

- *What Does The Character Need?* What are his inner needs—of which he may not even be conscious? What would bring him peace? What drives him? What makes him tick?

- *How Does The Character Do Things?* What are his limitations? What's his special knack? Can you define his approach? Can you define "his way"?

- *How Does The Character Think?* What are his standards? What are his principles? What are his values? How much is "too much" for him?

Okay, those were more than four questions.

The idea here is to develop the character freely. We want to get to know him in these four areas (his "wants," his "needs," his "doings," and his "thinking"). We want to get to know him completely so we can "map out" his nature, or get to know him through the *process* of mapping his nature.

What works for me in answering these questions is to take a moment to dream up my character and then write four scenes. For example:

- *Imagine the character writing a New Year's resolutions list or telling his life plans to another guy in a bar*—this scene answers "What does the character Want?"

- *Imagine an event of the character's backstory, the incident that marked him for life*—this scene answers "What does the character Need?"

- *Imagine the character doing some exceptional task, something that he'd never done before, and that puts him under unusual stress*—this scene answers "How does the character Do Things?"

- *Imagine the character making a decision under extreme pressure from his peers and love interests*—this scene answers "How does the character Think?"

Example

Let's do an example, shall we? Let's create a character named Johnny.

- **What does Johnny Want?** *Johnny talks to a Bartender and says, "Know what I'm gonna do? I'm gonna get me a boat, see? A sailboat, man, and just sail around the world. Gonna go to Tahiti, man, always wanted to go there. Gonna get me one of those digital cameras and send E-mail photos of me on the beach, a photo to everyone that didn't believe I could do it. Gonna show them my boat, man. Gonna send them pictures. To my ex, man, and to my boss. To my stupid boss that'll still be at his stupid desk, and still waiting for my stupid reports. He's gonna open his E-mail, and 'bang' he's gonna see me on Tahiti with the message 'still think I couldn't do it, jerk?' That's what I'm gonna do, man. That's what I'm gonna do."*

- **What does Johnny Need?** *"Johnny always thought he'd marry Jane, his high school sweetheart. Everybody in town thought it, too. The yearbook said so; the teachers thought so; his parents and her parents thought it, too. That's why when Johnny returned from college, he felt immediately that something was wrong. Everybody handled him with an annoying pity and the kind of reassurance that makes someone feel uneasy. It wasn't until his father told him the truth that he understood. Jane was pregnant with another guy's child. She was marrying the other guy, and that was that. Johnny turned bitter and cynical then and there. Instead of blaming Jane or himself, he blamed the whole town. Their insincere* *kindnesses, their compassionate deceit was, for him, the cause of his misfortune. Johnny abandoned his hometown soon after that night to never come back."*

- **How does Johnny Do Things?** *"Johnny comes home one evening to find a leak in the kitchen that's flooding his small apartment. Immediately, Johnny tries to find his tools, but the habitual mess of his home makes it impossible to find them. Johnny notices the puddle growing and abandons the search to seek out the water valve. He looks under the sink, but it's too dark to see anything. He tries to find a flashlight and finds none. The water keeps rising and Johnny thinks about calling a plumber. He finds the phone by tracing the cord on the wall, then looks for the phone book, but has no luck finding it. He notices the water still going up. Goes back to trying to close the main valve, but can't reach it under the sink. He tries calling the neighbor for help, but nobody's home. When Johnny stands still, trying to think of something else to fix it, the water starts spilling on the building stairs."*

- **How does Johnny Think?** *"Johnny is at a bar trying to impress a cute girl. He's almost got it when a gargantuan, drunken redneck trips over him and floods Johnny's new shirt with smelly cheap beer. Frenziedly, the mammoth drunk demands apologies from the astonished Johnny, who thinks for a moment between fighting this creature—and no doubt getting clobbered— or unfairly apologizing to him—and losing the young woman's admiration. He chooses to apologize, and unexpectedly, the girl declares to admire him more for this sudden burst of integrity."*

Now that we know more about our character, we can fire up our Dramatica software.

The idea behind all the prep work and scene drafting is now that we've seen our character in action, we can build him with ease and confidence. The characteristics on the screens won't be mere abstract ideas, but concrete words that describe the scenes we've created about our character.

Now, each of the questions connects directly with a particular "Set" of characteristics:

- *"What does the character Want?"* represents the character's *Purposes*.

- *"What does the character Need?"* stands for the character's *Motivations*.

- *"How does the character Do Things?"* corresponds to the character's *Methodology*.

- *"How does the character Think?"* speaks for the character's *Means of Evaluation*.

With the scene we've created on one hand and the "Build Characters" screens in front of us, we can start mapping the character's nature and make him consistent, yet complex.

Here we go:

- *Johnny's Purposes*: Let's see, I'll represent Johnny's desire to realize his lifelong dream of sailing to Tahiti with the purpose of *Actuality*. I'll use a purpose of *Aware* to show how he wants to send pictures to make everybody aware of his trip.

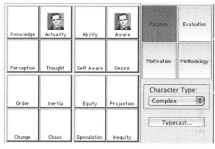

Johnny's Purposes

- *Johnny's Motivations*: From the anecdote, we gather Johnny needs to feel loved. I'll illustrate that with a motivation of *Feeling*. Johnny's objection to his peers' compassion towards him could be a motivation of *Oppose*.

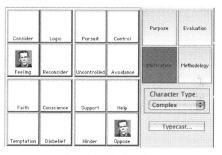

Johnny's Motivations

- *Johnny's Methodologies*: When Johnny tries to fix the leak, he makes it into an even bigger project than is necessary—a methodology of *Production*. Also, he constantly assesses the water level. That's a methodology of *Evaluation*.

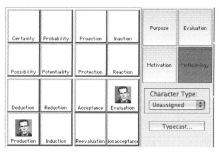

Johnny's Methodologies

- *Johnny's Means of Evaluation*:
  In the bar scene, Johnny
  chooses to end the quarrel with
  the drunk by apologizing—a
  means of evaluation of *Ending*.
  But he never gets to try to
  see if he could beat him. He
  accepts his own weakness
  without trying—a characteristic
  of *Trust*.

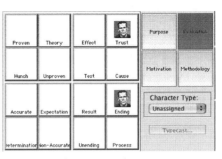

Johnny's Evaluations

That should do it.

There it lies before us, the complete map of a character's personality. His desires, drives, limitations and principles are complex enough to keep him interesting, but simple enough to make him consistent and true.

We've taken the first step in creating a great character, but we should keep in mind that it's only the first step. We now have to find how to transform these characteristics into events and material that will go in our screenplay. Sometimes we could use the scenes we've drafted for character exploration, but most times we'll have to tailor them to fit our story more precisely.

Meanwhile, let's go on with completing our character. We now have his inner personality, so let's give him a nice, appealing, external appearance.

7

APPEALING CHARACTERS

If you're like me, the part of a cake you enjoy most is the icing. But we've also found out that too much icing—or worse, pure icing— makes us sick. We found out that last one the hard way, didn't we?

Like a cake, a character needs two layers to be complete.

The dough of a character is his *Personality*—his inner drives, his desires, his limitations and principles. These are the traits that let a character stand and progress through the story. It is the magic wand that touches the audience's heart, makes them cry and fall in love with him.

The icing of a character is his *Characterization*—how he looks, who he hangs with, what he does for a living, his hobbies, if was he born on the right or wrong side of the tracks, if he's of noble descent, and so on. These qualities make a character more appetizing for the audience. These are the features the audience will recall more vividly when talking about the movie, the qualities that will inspire the best catchphrases and most colorful incidents, and of course, the items that are fun to write.

That's precisely their problem.

Just like icing on a cake, you can have too much of a good thing. It's common to find characters that are pure characterization and nothing else. Some scripts accurately describe a character's looks, friends, day job, pastimes, origins, and star sign, but say nothing about how he thinks, his wants, or what his true nature is. The audience quickly grows tired of these characters. It starts falling in love with their sincere qualities, but the second it discovers there's nothing beneath those layers of surface frosting, it starts hating him. "Why is the charming guy just standing there and doing nothing?" "What does he want out of life?" "I think he's an airhead." The viewers start wondering if it'd be too rude to walk out in the middle of the picture. Script Readers get rid of screenplays with characters like these even faster than the audience. Producers run from them like the plague.

The trick is not to avoid characterization, but to *find the right balance between characterization and personality*. Create a character with enough features to charm the viewers and a strong personality to move them. This is the Holy Grail of fictional persons, not easy to write, but this is what we're aiming for.

Dramatica has plenty of guidelines for creating Personality. The Build Character screens, the Character Type assignment, and the Character Typecast files are excellent tools to produce a finely structured character's soul. But, on the other hand, Dramatica has absolutely no rules on how to write the characterization. This lets us create it freely, without guidelines, and—since these external qualities

have no affect on the story's structure— it's better and more creative this way. Characterization obeys our artistic fancy.

Dramatica merely provides some space to jot the character's peculiarities on five screens titled: *Physical Traits, Affiliations & Beliefs, Skills, Interests,* and *Background.*

Because this is a book on creative methods, I'd like to share some of my personal favorites for crafting characterization. See if any of these inspire you in creating your own appealing characters.

Character Illustrating in the Dramatica Query System

Portray Someone You Know

This is a favorite of mine and other writers from the beginning of history. Characters have been named, described, profiled or inspired in many ways after the writers' relatives, friends, acquaintances, or enemies in almost every written story. (Note: A variation of this system would be the *Researched Character*. The writer interviews a real person who's a living example of the fictional person he's writing and puts his traits in the characterization). Some of the portrayed characters are copies of the source person. Others just take a trait or two and leave the rest to fantasy. Still others are composites of different folks, and thus, have the looks of the writer's uncle, but the beliefs of his best friend, the skills of an old army buddy, the interests of a neighbor, and the origins of that fifth grade bully that broke his nose in 1974.

The trouble in depicting people as characters is the risk of becoming infatuated with the characterization—thinking the audience will fall in love with the character just because she looks and talks like the writer's girlfriend. I advise always keeping the audience in mind.

Make the Character The Opposite Of The Cliché

Imagine a pirate: Eye patch, wooden leg, hook, beard, hat, and parrot on his shoulder. Now, imagine a pirate that looks the opposite of that cliché. What if our pirate was a cherub-faced teenager who's just as bloody and cruel as Blackbeard? Or a sixty-year-old, two hundred pound, Jamaican grandma who claims to have been Long John Silver's wet nurse?

Exploring the cliché's opposite can give us some interesting characters. However, the danger is going overboard and writing an implausible character ("A six-month-old baby pirate? Please!"). Keeping it real is the key.

Give The Audience What They Expect—but Insert Some Very Human Traits

Sometimes clichés are expected. Sometimes the audience won't accept a superhero who's not wearing a cape and tights, a secret agent that doesn't wear tuxedos and drive sports cars, or a scientist that's not wearing a white lab coat and talks with a central-European accent. It's better to give the audience what they want. However, these monolithic characters significantly improve by inserting a single human trait, a familiar weakness, or unexpected feature that drives them apart from the cliché. For example, a superhero that's allergic to pollen, a secret agent that never learned to drive a stick shift, an old Swedish scientist who's a huge James Brown fan and can reproduce every one of his moves...

Soon after the success of RAIDERS OF THE LOST ARK and super action hero *Indiana Jones'* fear of snakes, this cliché-with-human-trait practice was compulsory in screenwriting. It has since been overused. However, skillfully done, it still makes wonderful characters.

Make The Characterization The Opposite Of The Personality

This is tricky, but produces great traits. Imagine we have a character and already have mapped his personality: a *pursuing* motivation, a *proactive* methodology, an *effective* means of evaluation, and an *actual* purpose. He's an achiever, a real go-getter. What if he looked and behaved like the ultimate loser? What if he was a schmuck that, when the chips were down, would reveal the nature of a Hero?

This is useful for creating surprising characters and reinventing archetypes. The problem lies in understanding the character's nature to find its opposite. It is best to write some sketches of the character in action to understand his nature, and from those, find the opposite characterization.

There they are, four of my favorite ways to craft characterization. Are there any rules to it? Well, yes. *Don't Overdo It* and *Avoid The Clichés Whenever Possible*. The same rules for writing anything.

Now that we've developed our characterization in the Dramatica screens, how do we put it into the script? How do these physical traits, affiliations, skills, interests, and backgrounds go into the final screenplay?

To find out, let's look at each of them.

Physical Traits

This is where the writer has less control of the characterization. First, the director, producer, and designers all have a say on how the character should look. Their say-so usually has more weight than anything the screenplay says. Second, the more precise we are on describing a character, the more fine actors we exclude from performing that particular role. For these reasons, it's better to keep the physical description lean.

Usually, these traits are succinctly described within parentheses following the first introduction of a character. As a rule, the parentheses' contents are merely a number that states the character's age and a single descriptive sentence. The sentence describes the character *in a way that inspires the director, producer, and designers to achieve what the screenwriter has in mind.*

For example, "LISA (35. Beautiful in a Girl-Next-Door kind of way)" or "GARY (19. Too skinny to be a jock, so he compensates by wearing football jerseys all the time)."

One rule:

> **DON'T INCLUDE ANY MORE DESCRIPTION THAN IS STRICTLY NEEDED TO PICTURE THE CHARACTER IN YOUR MIND.**

Affiliations & Beliefs

About this trait, I find two kinds of characters: some that rely heavily on their affiliations and beliefs and some that, well, don't. The first type are people defined mostly by the company they keep, by the organizations they belong to, and the ones that hold their beliefs as banners. For example, the suburban kid that hangs out with inner-city thugs, or the arrogant MENSA cardholder that snubs everyone who can't pass her IQ test, or an intolerant fundamentalist that tries to convert you the moment he meets you.

The second type are... huh, everybody else.

For this second type of character, it is better to develop their affiliations and beliefs in the Dramatica software, but leave them out of the screenplay. Use them just to get to explore your character, to know him deeper, but don't bother the audience with unimportant facts.

Now, for the first type of characters, it is better to develop these traits as if they were part of his personality. Try to map them in the "Build Characters" screens. Expose these traits once in each act and, if possible, incorporate them into the plot or events—there's more on how to do this in upcoming chapters.

Skills

It is best to disclose skills in the first act as soon as we meet the character. If he reveals another skill later in the story—especially one that saves him from trouble— the audience feels cheated and the critics will shout "Deus Ex-Machina" in all their reviews. The sooner we learn the character's skills, the better.

James Bond, for example, is a character so skillful that he needs the complete first sequence of each of his movies just to reveal all that he can do. After the first dazzling display of skills, the audience believes any feat carried out by this character, and he can get away with saving the world with a pair of cuff links.

Interests

This is perhaps the most important trait of all. For some reason, the audience is immediately charmed by a character that openly states what he likes and does not like. This is the "he's just like me!" or "I know someone just like that!" force of the characterization.

It is not enough for a character merely to say what he likes; we must confirm it watching him explore his interests. So, if a character says he likes ice cream, put him in a scene relishing a triple scoop with hot fudge and two cherries. If she says she hates jazz, make her throw a complete Dizzy Gillespie collection out the window. If he says he's fond of soap operas, make him carefully set up the VCR to record the next day's episode of *"As The World Spins..."*

Use these unimportant but charming events to spice your scenes but don't give them too much weight. Less is more, as they say.

Background

This trait is the trickiest to insert in a screenplay: One misstep and we end up with one of those cliché background confessions that get in the way of the-plot, or worse, a flashback that exposes something that no one really cares about.

The best to do with backgrounds is to develop them just to get acquainted with our character. Include them in the script only if the occasion comes up, and if a part of the background can come out naturally in a scene.

So, basically, that's how I weave characterization into a screenplay. Am I forgetting something? Oh, of course, the main rule:

> **NEVER INTERRUPT THE NARRATIVE FLOW TO EXPOSE YOUR CHARACTERIZATION.**

When I've completed the first draft, I read it thoroughly, and if any characterization item feels out of place, I throw it away. Merciless as always.

We now have personality and characterization. What else is there to a character?

How about relationships? Let's see how a character interacts with another in the next chapter.

8

ENCODING CHARACTER RELATIONSHIPS

Before we continue, let me ask you an all-important question:

Why the heck are we doing all this anyway?

I mean, we have created the perfect Character—one with motivations, methodologies... the whole shebang. Now, how does this intricate personality make his way into the story? How do we show our perfect character to the audience? Here's how:

> **A** CHARACTER IS SHOWN BY HIS ACTIONS
> **AND DECISIONS UNDER PRESSURE.**

Easy, huh?

It's like this. Imagine a character that seems to be the Ultimate Generous Person. He gives money to charities every month, sponsors needy children in Uganda, donates a pint of blood every year, and what not. But, how is he going to act when the stakes are high? If, say, he gets in the middle of a nasty, vicious divorce and his wife claims the house, will he give it to her generously or will he struggle to keep it? How generous is he really, then?

Under pressure, a character reveals his true nature. If this character had a Motivation of "Help," he'll give his wife the house—even if she was a nasty witch. But if our character's Motivation is "Hinder," you'll bet he'll do anything to obstruct his wife's goals.

"High stakes" is an important part of how a character reveals his nature. The other important part is conflict. "Conflict" means, *the direct opposition between two characters' wills and the struggle this opposition causes*."

Bottom line:

> **A** CHARACTER CAN ONLY BE REVEALED BY
> **INTERACTING IN CONFLICT WITH OTHER CHARACTERS.**

We kind of expected that, didn't we?

But, wait, so far we've only built one character—the perfect character, yes, but only one— where do we get opposition?

Building Your Cast of Characters

Time has come for us to build our whole cast.

Since conflict is stronger between characters that have elements in the same **Quad** (we'll get to this later in this chapter), the best way to build a cast is to create first one character, and then form the personalities of the rest of our characters. The character usually created first is the Main Character.

(Note—If you are following this in your Dramatica software, set the Overall Story Domain to Manipulation to arrange the elements properly.)

Let's see how it's done.

(Go ahead, switch on your computer, start the Dramatica software, and open your "Build Characters" screen to follow this example. Done? Good).

Suppose we have character, Jane, who has a motivation of *Temptation*.

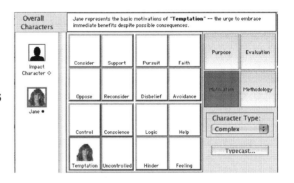

After we've created Jane and assigned her the *Temptation* element, we ask ourselves: Who has the biggest conflict with Jane? We take a moment to picture Jane having a loud argument or a bitter fight... with whom? Her husband? Okay, her husband it is. Let's create a character, Fred. Assign him to the element in the square *diagonally* opposed to Jane's *Temptation*. Characters in the diagonal relationship have the greatest potential for conflict.

Jane is Temptation; Fred is Conscience

Now Fred has a motivation of *Conscience*.

Keep in mind that up to now, Jane and Fred's disagreement is only about Jane's *Temptation* and Fred's *Conscience*. If we'd like to have Fred and Jane fighting over anything and everything, we must give Fred all the squares diagonally opposed to each of Jane's characteristics. But for now, let's stick to Jane's *Temptation* and all the conflict it creates.

Let's find a character that won't disagree with Jane's *Temptation*. To the contrary, let's find one who will consent to and even aid her temptation escapades. Again, let's take a moment to imagine Jane having a good time with her ideal Temptation-buddy... there! We've created the character, Mike, and he goes into the square *horizontally* aligned to Jane's *Temptation* square. We give Mike a motivation of *Uncontrolled*. Mike's freedom and wildness amplifies Janes drive to follow her temptations.

Now we need another character: one who doesn't agree with Jane's *Temptation*, but is necessary to make it happen, a character who's incompatible with Jane but required for her temptation. Let's imagine Jane tolerating an annoying character just because she promotes her *Temptation* moments... there! Let's add another character, Susan. She gets the element in the square *vertically* lined to Jane's *Temptation* square. We give Susan a motivation of *Control*.

A completed motivation quad

Now we have filled a motivation quad. It is always a good idea to work with complete quads. Doing so makes a more comprehensive story and gives all the possible opinions on the topics we're reviewing in our theme.

We should finish Jane's personality keeping in mind that we've got to fill every quad in which she has an element with the elements of the rest of our cast. This means that if Jane has a Purpose of *Desire*, Fred, Mike, and Susan's elements will be those surrounding *Desire*.

You have the choice to maintain Jane's relationship with each of the other characters. If you do this, Fred always has the element *diagonally* opposed to Jane's elements, so he always fights with her. Mike always has the element *horizontally* aligned to Jane, so they're always compatible. Susan always has the element *vertically* aligned to Jane, so they're always dependent on each other.

A completed purpose quad maintaining the relationships

A better alternative is to give Jane a complex and diverse relationship with the rest of the cast.

For instance, Jane has a big conflict with Fred over her *Temptation* motivation, but her *Pursuit* motivation complements Fred's *Disbelief* motivation; and her *Effect* evaluation amplifies Fred's *Accurate* evaluation. Jane's *Temptation* is compatible with Mike's *Uncontrolled* motivation, but her *Pursuit* motivation conflicts Mike's *Avoidance*, and so on.

The key here is to give variety to the characters' relationships. Keep them in the same quad as the Main Character's elements, but avoid keeping the same quad relationships. This makes them more interesting as characters.

Example motivation quad with alternate relationships: Jane conflicts with Mike, Jane complements Fred

Okay, then.

Let's review. Relationships are the key to the character's personality, and since a nature can only be exposed by interactions, relationships and personality become one. The character's inner self is defined by the people with whom he relates and vice versa.

This means that our cast should be imagined as a *whole*. Their personalities should be built in a way that allows them to interact with one another.

Sometimes, the best way to do this is to create the character's relationships first and build their personalities from that relationship. For example, Jane and Fred have a "Marriage on the Rocks" rapport, from which we build their personalities mostly based on conflicting elements. Other times it is best to build the characters first and then create a relationship based on what we've built. Susan and Fred have mostly *horizontally* paired elements, called **Companion Pair** elements, so we can give them a relationship of close friendship. Any particular method can or cannot work for you. What works for me is to develop the characters separately. I write scene sketches and all the things discussed in chapter six, *True Character*. I then tweak their personalities to make their elements fit into relationships. Weird, huh? The key here is to experiment and develop your own way of merging personalities and relationships.

But now…

When we have a fully built cast, it is time to develop and expand the characters' relationships. Let's start by asking what bond exists between two particular characters? Are they friends or foes? Hypocrites or sincere confidants? What's the basis of their liaison? To what extreme will it go? Will they die for each other or are they just fair weather friends? When we have the answer to these questions, we should write some scenes sketches to see each correlation.

With a solid idea of the relationships, we can give each one a title. For example, we title Jane and Fred's relationship, "Marriage on the Rocks". Let's scribble our titles in the Character's Relationships screens at the Query System in the Dramatica software.

And while we're here in the software, let's click the Reports icon and open the Build Characters report. It is a description of our characters' elements and how they interact with one another. It reads something like this:

> *"Jane's motivation of Temptation is in conflict with Fred's motivation of Conscience, amplified by Mike's motivation of Uncontrolled, and diminished by Susan's motivation of Control."*

There lay our characters' natures and how to show them—their conflicts, how they're going to decide under pressure, and how they're going to act eventually to change the course of the story. In the Build Characters report lies the characters' soul, trapped inside a rough rock of cold, abstract elements. We just have to illustrate those elements, find the correct examples and pull their spirits out into the light, bring them around, and expose them to the audience.

Character Relationships

Time to complete our characters' relationships:

The tools we'll use are our "Build Characters" report (so let's print it), and the sketches and previous material we've developed about our characters' relationships.

Let's bring it all together. Ready? Go:

First, *separate the elements of each relationship.* Take the Build Character Report and cross out the elements of all the characters except the two involved in the chosen relationship. If we're starting with Jane and Fred's relationship, we'll cross out each of Mike and Susan's elements. We'll end up with something like this:

> *Jane and Fred's Relationship: "Marriage on the Rocks"*

> *Jane's motivation of Temptation is in conflict with Fred's motivation of Conscience.*

> *Jane's motivation of Pursuit is diminished by Fred's motivation of Disbelief.*

> *Jane's methodology of Reevaluation is in conflict with Fred's methodology of Evaluation.*

> *Jane's methodology of Possibility is in conflict with Fred's methodology of*

Probability.

Jane's means of evaluation in terms of Effect is amplified by Fred's means of evaluation in terms of Accurate.

Jane's purpose of Desire is diminished by Fred's purpose of Projection.

Nice. Each paragraph above describes a character interaction. The elements depict how each character decides and acts (Jane acts Temptingly while Fred acts Consciously, of course); and the comparison term (*Conflict, Diminished, Amplified*) describes what kind of interaction these personalities have.

Let me translate these Dramatica terms into more sensible, "creative-writing-class" terms:

- **Conflict** means the characters *fight one another* over these topics.

- **Amplified** means the characters are *compatible with one another* in these topics.

- **Diminished** means these topics make the characters *codependent or somehow addicted to one another*.

So, to illustrate each interaction, we just go back to our Relationship Title ("Marriage on the Rocks") and just ask three questions:

- What does *Character A's element* have to do with *The Relationship's Title*? (*What does Jane's Temptation have to do with this Marriage on the Rocks?*)

- What does *Character B's element* have to do with *The Relationship's Title*? (*What does Fred's Conscience have to do with this Marriage on the Rocks?*)

- How does *Character A's element* and *Character B's element* interact with each other? (*How do Jane's Temptation and Fred's Conscience fight each other?*)

Answer each of them. Take a moment to imagine a dramatic response for each question and jot them on a piece of paper:

- What does Jane's Temptation have to do with this Marriage on the Rocks?

  "Jane is a compulsive flirt."

- What does Fred's Conscience have to do with this Marriage on the

Rocks?

"Fred is self-restraining to the point of acting cold and indifferent to his wife. This behavior makes Jane feel unloved."

- How do Jane's Temptation and Fred's Conscience make Jane and Fred fight each other?

"Jane flirts with other guys to irritate Fred but Fred refuses to show emotion—any emotion—and appears cold and indifferent."

Create a paragraph that describes the complete interaction as a scene:

"Every time they go out, Jane flirts with some other guy, trying to make Fred jealous. She feels unloved by her seemingly apathetic husband and tries to incite some passion in him. Fred remains unmoved by her display and Jane gets furious, eventually feeling insulted by her husband's indifference."

Illustrate all the interactions in the relationship the same way. The idea is to describe them as if we were telling a story. Describe each interaction as if it was a moment of the characters' intimate life. Perhaps not presented in order of beginning to end, all those events portray their personal relationship as a whole.

Let's try it:

- **Jane's motivation of Pursuit is diminished by Fred's motivation of Disbelief.** What do Jane's Pursuit and Fred's Disbelief have to do with this failing marriage, and how do these topics make Jane and Fred addicted to each other?

"Eventually Jane goes ahead and has an affair. She lets her husband indirectly know of this, but he doesn't believe it. They start a sick game where she leaves proof of her infidelity and he dismisses it."

- **Jane's methodology of Reevaluation is in conflict with Fred's methodology of Evaluation.** What do Jane's Reevaluation and Fred's Evaluation have to do with this failing marriage, and how do these topics make Jane and Fred fight each other?

"Jane reevaluates her marriage and thinks about a divorce. Fred was raised a catholic and evaluates the divorce as unacceptable. They argue about it, but never agree."

- **Jane's methodology of Possibility is in conflict with Fred's methodology of Probability.** What do Jane's Possibility and Fred's Probability have to do with this failing marriage, and how do these topics make Jane and Fred fight each other?

"Jane suggests a second honeymoon as a possibility to fix differences between them. Fred rejects the idea, considering that harmony is just not probable. She gets mad because he's not giving the reconciliation a chance."

- **Jane's means of evaluation in Terms of Effect is amplified by Fred's means of evaluation in terms of Accurate.** What do Jane's Effect evaluation and Fred's Accurate evaluation have to do with this failing marriage, and how do these topics make Jane and Fred compatible with each other?

  "Jane evaluates their sex life as a failure since she can't get the effect she wants on her husband. However, Fred considers this bland sex life okay. Somehow, Jane finds comfort in knowing her husband is satisfied with his love life and thinks twice about leaving him and looking for another man."

- **Jane's purpose of Desire is diminished by Fred's purpose of Projection.** What do Jane's Desire and Fred's Projection have to do with this failing marriage, and how do these topics make Jane and Fred addicted to each other?

  "Jane desires a successful marriage. Fred just wants to stop it from getting worse. Neither of them can do anything to fix their marriage or to end it, so they keep it as it is, even though it harms them."

Okay.

Each of the paragraphs sketches a piece of the characters' natures, revealing clearly how the characters decide and act under pressure and the conflict their decisions give them. Jane and Fred are both complex characters with defects as well as redeeming qualities. They try to do their best to solve their problems and to save what's left of their marriage, the most important objective in their lives.

Together, these paragraphs describe the characters' personalities and tell the whole story of their relationship. It'd be just a matter of giving them the correct order and then placing them into the rest of the story to reveal these complex characters to our audience.

How do we do this? How do we take all we've created here and incorporate it into our screenplay? Let's look at the next chapter to find out.

9

EXPOSING CHARACTER EVENTS

Writing with Dramatica is a process of gradual liberation. Our characters usually start imprisoned in small, abstract ideas like "Motivation of Consider," or "Purpose of Knowledge." From there, we illustrate those ideas to release our characters from the abstract realm. We give them relationships to set them free of their individual prisons, and we describe the relationships' interactions to bring our characters into the world, to turn those cold, abstract elements into scene material.

Eventually, our characters live in descriptive interactions like this:

> *"Suze considers going after the killer by herself, but Lieutenant Washington struggles to make her reconsider."*

That's okay. It can be used as scene material, represents the characters' decisions, and has enough conflict to make it interesting. But it's still not good enough for the screenplay. Now, how do we turn this illustration into a real scene? How do we infuse life force in this paragraph to turn our intangible characters into living, breathing, fictional beings?

Here's how:

> **TO GIVE LIFE TO OUR CHARACTERS WE HAVE TO INSERT THEM INTO OUR STORY.**

A character cannot stand alone. He can't breathe and live without a story that puts him in action. Just as he needs another character's opposition to reveal his nature, he needs a story to put it to a test. The audience needs the story to know how the character reacts to the plot events, theme issues and genre environment to understand him fully, to recognize him as a fictional person and to identify with him.

Let's say we have our characters "Suze" and "Lieutenant Washington" as part of this story:

*"Suze is a redeemed prostitute that finds herself in the path of a
Serial Killer. Lieutenant Washington is a detective with stiff moral
principles and a certain bias against prostitutes. He is assigned to
protect Suze."*

Okay, suppose we've already developed Suze and Lt. Washington. We've built
their personalities, dreamed up their characterization, created and illustrated their
relationship, and ended with the interaction where Suze considers going after the
killer and Washington struggles to make her reconsider.

Suppose that, on the side, we've developed the complete story about the serial
killer. Its theme, plot, and genre are thoroughly elaborated. We've storyformed it,
storyencoded it, outlined it, and ended up with around forty-eight scenes that tell
this saga from beginning to end. Now, how do we weave the characters' interactions
into our screenplay?

Basically, there are two ways. The first—and more obvious— would be to *write
a whole new scene for your characters' interaction.* Develop any given interaction as
its own scene with its own setting, period of time and extension; with its own slug
lines, actions, and dialogue—from "CUT TO" to "CUT TO." Then, insert it in any
chosen place of your story.

Like this:


```
EXT.  SUZE'S BUILDING - NIGHT

LT. WASHINGTON stands guard on the sidewalk with
a serene, watchful attitude.  SUZE comes out of
the building with a nervous step, discovers
Lt. Washington, and approaches him, disguising
her anxiety.

          SUZE
     You still here?  Where's
     your replacement?

          LT. WASHINGTON
     He's late.  I'm taking his
     shift.

Suze sighs to hide a loud curse and turns to go
back into the building.  Lt. Washington stops
her abruptly holding her arm.

          LT. WASHINGTON
     Open your purse
     immediately!
```

                         SUZE
                What the—?

                              LT. WASHINGTON
                Think you can hide a gun
                from a cop?

He grabs her purse and opens it.

                         SUZE
                What makes you think you
                have the right to—

He extracts a small revolver and shows it to
her. Suze lowers her sight with anger.

                              LT. WASHINGTON
                You were thinking of going
                after him, weren't you?

She bites her lip, trembling with frustration.

                              LT. WASHINGTON
                Don't you realize the
                danger? You think you even
                have the slightest chance
                to—

                         SUZE
                What other chance have I
                got? Waiting for you to
                screw up again and let him
                kill me like the others?

Lt. Washington stares at her silently. Then
pockets the gun.

                              LT. WASHINGTON
                He won't get to you. I
                promise.

He escorts the furious Suze back into the
building.

    The advantage of developing a character's interaction as a scene is that we bring
more emphasis to our characters' natures. This is great for **Ensemble Stories** (THE

BIG CHILL), some **Dramas** and any film that stresses character over plot, theme, or genre. The disadvantage is that we increase the number of scenes in our script (its locations, incidental roles, and overall costs). Some genres (such as **Action Movies**, **Thrillers**, and **Comedies**) can't take that much emphasis on character, especially in scenes like the one above which have no real "turning point" (the central event that advances the plot in every scene). They feel empty, too expository, and uninteresting.

The remedy for the disadvantage would be to opt for the other way to weave character interactions. This would be:

Weave Your Character Interactions Into Your Existing Scenes

This is much more subtle. The idea is to dedicate only a couple of scene "beats" (some actions, a little dialogue, a few visual elements...) to that particular character interaction. Arrange the character moment as a part of the scene, as a path to the "turning point" or as a reaction to it.

To do this we must first:

Identify The Central Event Of Each Of Our Scenes

The Central Event (*Turning Point*) is what the scene is all about. It's the action or revelation that changes the course of the story, and it defines the scene subject (I discuss this at length in the chapters on Plot in Section V of this book).

Having identified all our central events, we can list them into a step outline of our scenes. With that outline we can:

Choose The Scene In Which The Interaction Should Go

This is an aesthetic choice. To find it we'd go through the scenes listed in our step outline until we find a scene that creates the perfect environment for a particular interaction. Genre and style are considered here, but the main lines in choosing a scene to insert an interaction are:

- **Similarity**. In this case the Scene's Central Event can be easily related to the Interaction's Subject. Let's say we find a scene with a Central Event of:

  "Suze finds out the police's strategies to find the killer have been ineffective so far, and they're at the point of declaring the case unresolved and closed."

  It is easy to link this scene to the event where Suze wants to go after the killer by herself. The event would go naturally and effortlessly in here.

- **Contrast**. Conversely, the aim here is to find a Scene that's unlike the given interaction, a Central Event that creates an interesting conflict with the matter of the characters' moment. Let's say we have the following scene:

  "Even though Lt. Washington knows Suze used to be a prostitute, he starts falling in love with her."

  The connection between this scene and the interaction is much more subtle and difficult to write, but it would create a deep impact in the audience if Lt. Washington is forced to reveal his feelings as the only way of making Suze reconsider.

Having chosen a scene for our interaction, we are ready to weave it. For this we need a scene previously developed, outlined, or drafted in some way. With the scene draft in our hands we could:

Locate The Point In The Scene Where The Interaction Should Go

Is it before, or after the Central Event? Is the interaction a source for the Turning Point (*Suze first considering going after the killer, and then forcing Lt. Washington to reveal his feelings for her*), or is it an upshot of it (*Suze first finding out the police are about to shut the case down, and then deciding to go after the killer*).

With this decided, we are now ready to:

Weave It

To "weave it" means to "write it." We're about to write the first draft of the characters' interaction, to turn our conceptual illustration into a real screenplay, and to finish the process of creating living, breathing characters.

Writing is a matter of personal talent and, mostly, practice. So the idea here is to write it, consider it, rewrite it, expose it, rewrite it, pitch it, rewrite it.

However, some guidelines can be valuable in writing a character interaction. Here they are:

There are three ways of exposing an interaction, or any other dramatic item for that matter:

- *Dialogue*. This is the simplest way to expose it. The characters just state their decisions in straightforward speeches.

```
                SUZE
     I'm going after the killer,
     and there's nothing you can
     do to stop me.
```

```
          LT. WASHINGTON
     I can lock you up, if
     that's what it takes to
     make you change your mind.
```

Dialogue is a short, economical, and clear way to expose the characters'
natures. But its disadvantage is that it is too trivial. Talk is cheap. The
audience may take what a character says as insignificant.

There's another way:

- **Visuals**. This works by translating the characters' elements into
  movements, images, and deeds. We see the character putting his nature
  into practice, the concrete opposition of the other character, and the
  struggle resulting of this. For example:

```
EXT.  STREET - DAY

Lt. Washington escorts Suze down a busy street
when suddenly she sees the Killer turning a
corner on the opposite sidewalk.  The Killer
notices her, sees the cop at her side, makes a
quick decision, and runs away.

Suze turns quickly to Washington, but realizing
he's unaware of the Killer, she quickly grabs
the lieutenant's gun and runs to follow the
killer.

The Lieutenant is stunned for a second before
going after her.

Suze loses the killer in a dark alley. Clutching
the gun, she vigilantly searches among trash
cans and cardboard boxes when a hand comes out
of a dark corner, seizes the gun and gives her a
powerful shove that throws her to the pavement.

Terrified, Suze looks up at her aggressor and
finds Lt. Washington, holstering his gun,
staring sternly and extending a hand to help her
up to her feet.
```

This is much more powerful than dialogue because cinema is a visual
medium. The only problem here is that visual elements may carry too

much power and thus seem more important than the scene's event, giving a sense of "false suspense" if not used properly.

- **Subtext**. "Subtext" means *whatever is said without words or actions*. In a screenplay, subtext is achieved by creating a situation where the audience can guess what the characters are thinking. In a character interaction, the characters won't talk about their personalities—nor would they do anything to reveal them— but they will talk and act about issues that unwillingly will expose their desires, drives, principles, or limitations.

Example:

```
INT. SUZE'S BEDROOM - NIGHT.

The room is a mess.  Suze searches frantically
through her drawers and closets without finding
what she's looking for.  She's desperate and
quietly furious.

Lt. Washington opens the door and sees her.

                    LT. WASHINGTON
               What's the matter?

Suze keeps looking, but hides her irritated
state.

                    SUZE
               Nothing.

Lt. Washington puts his hand in his own pocket
and brings out a SMALL REVOLVER.

                    LT. WASHINGTON
               Looking for this?

Suze sees the gun and blushes.  Lt. Washington
pockets it again.

                    LT. WASHINGTON (CONT'D)
               Don't even think about it.
               It's crazy.

                    SUZE
               I have no choice.
```

```
Lt. Washington kneels beside Suze and helps her
put her things back in the drawer.

                    LT. WASHINGTON
              Of course you do.

He closes the drawer with a firm slam.
```

Subtext is an elegant and meaningful way of exposing interactions and dramatic items. It creates deep emotional impact in the audience and allows the actors and director to expose their talents at their best.

The problem with subtext is—of course— that it relies too much on the actors' and directors' abilities. Subtext elements are incomprehensible if not performed properly. For example, Lt. Washington kneeling beside Suze to help her which means that she has the choice of letting him catch the killer, or him slamming the drawer which means he won't let her look for the killer by herself.

Deciding the way to expose a character's interaction is a matter of balance. Does the story need more emphasis on character at this point or does it need less? Is a minor bit of dialogue required now, or should I tell the complete scene with visual elements? Do my genre and target audience accept this much subtext, or should I be more direct?

Resolve these questions by trying different approaches and seeing which works best (writing and rewriting as always). It's fun to imagine different ways to expose the same scene. Watching your characters in different scenarios helps you visualize them, and love them. After all, that's what a character is for.

We've completed the process of creating a character, from conception to actual writing. Now, let's look at a nifty trick to expand our characters even further.

10

CHARACTER RELATIONSHIPS AS SUBPLOTS

"So much to tell, so little time!"—That could be the catchy chorus for a song entitled "*The Screenwriter's Blues.*"

And it's true. Every screenwriter can tell you the problem with feature-length scripts is that they are too short. Even if they are 200-page/3-hour/double-DVDers, screenplays just are not long enough to explore in full the plot's ramifications or the characters' personalities. Never will a movie portray a character with the exquisite detail of a novel. Never will a flick develop its plot to the colossal span of a saga. Never will we, poor screenwriters, break the confinement of the feature-length script and the scarce dramatic items that we can present to the audience in two hours.

Or could we?

The solution for fitting big stories into brief screenplays is giving characters' relationships a double function. Do not only use relationships to reveal the characters' natures and conflicts, but give them the added task of exposing a story line, the extra chore of developing complementary subjects and expanding the theme to the fullest. This method can condense the massive complexities of THE BROTHERS KARAMAZOV to an extent that fits nicely into a 120-page script without missing a single "troika."

But, isn't this condensing method too tricky? How can we make sure we're not leaving out too much dramatic stuff or confusing the audience? Is this system too complicated?

Well... nah. Dramatica makes it effortless.

Let's see how it's done.

First we have to define our subplot by separating it from the central plot and identifying its own subject. Let's say we're writing a **Social Drama** about the death penalty and life in prison in general. Our central plot is about an inmate on death row, but we'd like to develop a subplot about forgiveness, a little parallel story about two inmates in the same block with a mortal grudge. One of them killed the other's brother in a gang war— a little story with tough guy interactions and a redeeming conclusion.

So, having identified the basic idea for our subplot, we'll develop it. Let's start by giving the subplot a beginning, middle, and end. This will give us an idea of how we would like it to go. Let's say:

> *"With great expectation, an inmate learns the guy who killed his brother is being transferred to his own cell block. He makes all sorts of preparations and plans to avenge his brother, but when the other guy comes in, he finds out that killing him is not as easy as he thought. They both engage in a lengthy game of life and death that ends in the first prisoner forgiving his brother's killer."*

Okay, that's enough for a rough outline.

Next we find our two suitable characters to act this subplot. Let's choose *Julio* and *Raoul*—two incidental characters we created earlier in the central plot. Will they do? Yup, those two are the characters for this tale.

Now it is time to structure the subplot. Since it has a double duty as a character relationship, we'll structure it with the characters' elements. The trick is to build the characters according to the subplot synopsis. We have to analyze it and translate each action, each desire, each aim and statement into a Character Element that builds their natures.

The easiest way to do this is to start with just one character and then build the other according to the elements of this first one. Let's start with Julio since he's better defined in the synopsis:

- Julio has a *Motivation of Consider,* since he's considering to avenge his brother; he also has a *Motivation of Feeling*, since all his hate is motivated by the love of his brother.

- Julio has a *Methodology of Proaction*, since he takes the first action in the brawl.

- Julio has a *Means of Evaluation of Ending*, since he evaluates the only way of ending his grudge is killing the other guy.

- Julio has a *Purpose of Self-Aware*, since he can't see any other objective than his own desires. He also has a *Purpose of Equity*, since he believes his revenge obeys his particular idea of justice.

  That should do it.

Time to build Raoul. We'll do our second character in a different way. This time let's start by thinking of the relationship we'd like him to have with the first character. Since Raoul is Julio's sworn enemy, many of Raoul's elements would be chosen to be in *conflict* with Julio's. They also share a sick game of violence, so several of their elements would be *codependent* (vertically aligned) to each other.

Let's build Raoul. If you'd like to follow this in your Dramatica software, set the OS Domain to *Fixed Attitude* to arrange the elements properly. Here we go:

- Let's give Raoul a *Motivation of Reconsider* so he can be in conflict with Julio's motivation of Consider. We'll also give Raoul a *Motivation of Control* that is codependent with Julio's motivation of Feeling.

- Let's give Raoul a *Methodology of Reaction* to be in conflict with Julio's methodology of Proaction.

- Let's give Raoul a *Means of Evaluation of Unending* to be in conflict with Julio's Means of Evaluation of Ending.

- Let's give Raoul a *Purpose of Ability*, to make it codependent with Julio's purpose of Self-Aware. We'll also give Raoul a *Purpose of Inequity* and make it conflict with Julio's Purpose of Equity.

That's it. Now to describe it.

The secret here is to make each interaction a moment of the subplot. To transform each character conflict into an event that, together, will recount the synopsis we've written for our subplot.

So, let's reread our synopsis, print a Build Characters report, and take a moment to imagine how each interaction can illustrate a scene of our subplot. Keep in mind that these scenes won't be created in "beginning to end" order. We will arrange them after we've created them.

Let's see:

> *"Julio's motivation of Consider is in conflict with Raoul's motivation of Reconsider"*—this could be a scene where Raoul changes Julio's considerations by saying that killing him won't bring his brother back.

> *"Julio's motivation of Feeling is diminished by Raoul's motivation of Control"*—this could be the scene when Julio first sees Raoul and Raoul's controlled attitude enrages Julio's feelings even further.

> *"Julio's methodology of Proaction is in conflict with Raoul's methodology of Reaction"*—this could be Julio's first action to kill Raoul, Raoul's violent response and the fight that develops from there.

> *"Julio's means of evaluation in terms of Ending is in conflict with Raoul's means of evaluation in terms of Unending"*—this could be an early scene where Julio first hears that Raoul is being transferred to his block. Julio—who thought he was over his brother's murder—feels the same

anger again and thinks the only way to end it is to kill his brother's murderer.

"Julio's purpose of Self-Aware is diminished by Raoul's purpose of Ability"—this could be a scene where Julio realizes that Raoul is a better fighter and he starts feeling unworthy of exacting his brother's revenge. From there Julio gets depressed and even suicidal.

"Julio's purpose of Equity is in conflict with Raoul's purpose of Inequity"—this could be when Julio starts thinking that killing his brother's killer won't make things fair, and will be just another injustice.

Enough for our subplot.

So we see, the moment we structure our subplot with character elements, it starts showing more depth, becoming more interesting and complete. The characters' motives and reasons become clear now that we know that Julio spares his enemy's life. Julio starts thinking that murdering him won't bring his brother back, and the turning points are more obvious now that we have an idea of Julio's character arc.

At this point, we may be tempted to write a couple of extra scenes that complete our subplot. That can be done, but keep in mind the key quality of a subplot is its lack of detail. Making a subplot too comprehensive turns it into an alternate plot that competes for attention with the main story. This would be okay if we're aiming for the **Ensemble Genre**, but if not, it'd be better to keep these complementary scenes to a minimum.

Okay, it is time to Storyweave our scenes. We'll start by giving them an order that resembles our original synopsis. Some of the scenes will have an obvious place in this arrangement, others will be more uncertain. Try experimenting with different arguments and see which makes the most interesting story.

After defining an order, we're ready to insert the subplot into the first draft of our script. Here we have to consider if our illustrated interactions are going in as scenes of their own (with their own location, time and extension) or if they are just "subplot moments," placed in the middle of another scene.

Let's try our first alternative:

```
INT. PRISON LIBRARY - DAY

JULIO mops the floor while a GUARD watches idly.

RAOUL enters with the BOOK CART.  Immediately
Julio tenses and sticks his hand in his pocket
to hold a hidden shank.  The Guard becomes wary
and fixes his gaze on both.
```

Raoul notices Julio, then notices the Guard
staring and smiles sarcastically. He starts
organizing the books on their shelves while
Julio manages to mop closer to him, still
holding the shank.

>   JULIO
>   You think you're macho?
>   I'll see you when the
>   hack's not looking.

>   RAOUL
>   As you wish, bato.

Julio looks at the Guard and sees he's still
watching them. Julio clutches the shank harder.

>   RAOUL
>   But believe me, bato, as
>   macho as you may be, it
>   won't bring your brother
>   back.

Perplexed, Julio looks at Raoul expecting a
sneering smile, but Raoul's face is serious and
serene.

Julio holds his breath for a second...releases
the shank and moves away from Raoul.

   Or, a more subtle alternative is to take that same interaction and insert it as part
of another scene:

INT. PRISON'S TV HALL - NIGHT

Some inmates watch TV using headphones. JONES
(an inmate) wanders in and stares at the screen
where an anchorwoman delivers the news. An
electronic image of the prison front wall
appears behind her.

Jones approaches WALKER—another inmate who
watches with his headphones.

>   JONES
>   Yo, Walker, what up?

Walker ignores him.

> JONES
> Man, what they're sayin?

Without looking away, Walker answers him.

> WALKER
> They've invented a new
> lethal injection. They're
> using it here first.

> JONES
> Man, why they want a new
> injection? Death is death,
> ain't it?

JULIO, who was watching TV from a corner, takes
off his headphones to comment:

> JULIO
> Put a punk here a few
> years, it'll kill him for
> sure. Don't need no new
> injection.

Julio places his headphones back on with
difficulty. Jones comments while staring
blankly at the screen.

> JONES
> 'sides, nothin's gonna
> bring back this guy's
> victim, huh?

Julio hears this and stops cold with the
headphones in his hands.

From the corner of his eye, he checks out RAOUL—
who's at another corner of the hall checking him
out in turn.

Julio lowers his sight and tries to put his
headphones back on. He hesitates and finally
yanks them furiously, tosses them on the floor
and steps out.

Raoul looks at them for a moment, then returns
to stare fixedly at the TV with the rest of the

```
inmates.  A picture of a death-row inmate has
appeared now on the screen...
```

You get the idea: Different approaches give different emphasis to our subplots. The only way to discover the precise emphasis a subplot needs is to write several drafts and see which one works best.

Okay, through the last several chapters we've developed our characters extensively. Now it is time to extensively develop the rest of our story. That's what we'll do in the following section.

SECTION IV
DEVELOPING
THE STORY

THE SEVERAL
DRAMATICA PATHS

11

STEP-BY-STEP DEVELOPMENT

Dramatica's StoryGuide is a progressive method for creative writing, a tutorial of Dramatica's principles, and a lifesaver when you have to develop a complete story from some minimal ideas and nil materials.

Suppose you are in a predicament such as this:

Your agent calls you for an urgent meeting today at lunch. In the middle of the meal, he puts next to your Reuben Sandwich an 8 x 10 glossy of a little known actor and says:

"Remember him? He was in 'Titanic.' He played the waiter who didn't drown. Anyway, the studio is very interested in launching his career, in making him a star, and we want you to write the vehicle that will put him right up there. We'd love see him in a *Spy Thriller*, an *Intrigue/Drama* story that shows his exceptional acting abilities. We want it to be action-packed but profound at the same time, explosive but also philosophical—think John Le Carré, think Tom Clancy. Are we on the same page here? Good. When can I see an outline—better yet, a short treatment? Fifteen days? I knew I could trust in you."

And without even letting you answer, he signs the check and steps out.

Well, at least he signed the check.

Now, what could you do to write this hasty treatment based on these meager ideas?

Well, you could start by going home, turning on your computer and opening the StoryGuide Screen on your Dramatica software.

Let's go through it together to see how these skimpy ideas, these series of abstract demands and vague references, develop into true writing material, and into solid ideas to complete a treatment in fifteen days.

Okay. Since we have little time, we'll use the *Level One StoryGuide,* which is the fastest path.

The first—and most important—thing to consider is that *Nothing That We Write Is Etched In Stone.* This is a creative process. We go back and forth, writing and rewriting, fixing and improving what we create until we reach something good enough for our treatment.

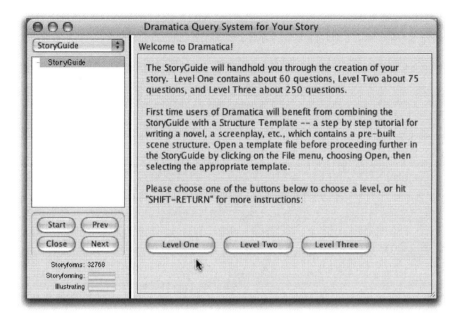

Story Title

Take the first question in the StoryGuide: *"What's The Title Of Your Story?"* We don't know enough about our story to give it a good—or even a decent—title. So, we give it a working label just to identify it, such as, "Spy Thriller" or "Actor's Vehicle"—anything that differentiates this story from the rest of our projects.

Let's go to the next question.

Story Logline

We don't know enough about our story to tell a Logline with a beginning, a middle, and end. So, we write down everything we know about this project in the logline. We summarize the requested qualities and turn them into writing material. We first jot down:

> *"This is a Spy Thriller with an emphasis on dramatic situations and a philosophical twist."*

That's a good start. Then we remember the agent mentioned John Le Carré and Tom Clancy, so we note:

> *"The plot turns around a conspiracy, a scheme centered on an intelligence agency of dubious morals. There's some government treason and patriotic duplicity. Military secrets are involved as well as covert plans for some nuclear weapon (a submarine, perhaps?)."*

Not much of a logline, but it has all the needed elements present.

Plot Synopsis

"Plot Synopsis" is our next question. We leave it blank for now. We'll get back to this when we know more about our story.

Creating Characters

The next couple of questions are about *"Creating Characters."* What do we know about our characters? Well, since we're writing a spy thriller, our *Main Character* should be a secret agent of some sort, and since we're writing a vehicle, he'll be played by the actor we saw in the photo at lunch. We'll create our Main Character based on those two traits. His "working name" is "Nick" after the actor who'll be playing him. His *Description* is similar to what we saw in the photo. His *Activities* are suitable for a spy:

> *"Nick works gathering and analyzing sensitive data for an Intelligence Agency."*

That's all we know about our Main Character at this point.

We leave the questions about our *"Impact Character"* blank since we don't know enough to create it. We'll come back later to craft this character.

Story Goal

Next, the StoryGuide takes us to the *Storyforming* part. It starts by asking, *"What's The Goal In Your Story?"* It's too soon to identify a definitive goal, but we can guess based on what we've developed so far:

> *"The goal revolves around a sensitive and dangerous piece of information."*

Ambiguous, but this brief description of the goal gets us closer to our final objective.

The Overall Story Domain

Next come a series of questions about the Throughlines and Domains. The first one is about the *Overall Story.* Here we make a selection based on our genre and the request for an "action-packed" script:

> *"The Overall Story Domain is Activities."*

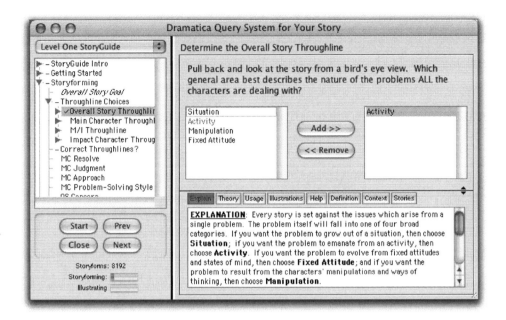

Good enough. Still, the next question, *"Give examples of how all the characters are involved in Activities or Endeavors"* will remain blank until we know more about our story.

The Main Character Domain

The next question is about the *Main Character Domain (Throughline)*. We can choose between *A Situation* and *A Fixed Attitude*. Let's choose *Situation* to put him into a dangerous predicament. We even start illustrating it with whatever stems from the character's activities:

> *"Nick is an American agent operating undercover in a hostile country."*

The Impact Character and Subjective Story Domains

The next two throughlines have been chosen automatically by the program: *Subjective Story Domain (M/I Throughline) of Manipulations*— which we don't know enough to illustrate yet —and *Impact Character Domain of Fixed Attitude*. For the Impact Character Domain, the illustration comes naturally after what we've developed earlier. If Nick is in a hostile country, the fixed attitude of his opposite character must reflect the country's hostility. The Impact Character must embody the difference between Nick's attitude and the country he's infiltrating. Let's say this character is a Russian who still believes in the idealistic view of Communism. I like this choice because it gives the character a romantic "cold-war" charm and accentuates the similarities with Le Carré's earlier works. We'll develop this character in detail later.

Character Dynamics Choices

Let's go on with our storyform. Some of our choices are made according to the impression we want to make on our audience, while others are purely aesthetic choices. Let's see:

- For *MC Resolve*, we choose *Change* to redeem our character of any possible wrongdoings he may commit.

- For *MC Judgment*, we choose *Good* to create a sensation of a happy ending in the audience.

- The *MC Approach* is already chosen as *Do-er* by the software, which relieves us from making this choice.

- For *MC Problem-Solving Style (Mental Sex)*, we choose *Intuitive* just because we'd like to see our analytical secret agent using intuition to solve his most complex troubles.

Plot, Theme, and Other Choices Remaining

Other storyform choices are made according to what we've developed so far, and how we'd like it to be further developed.

- We have four choices for the *Overall Story Concern: "Understanding, Doing, Obtaining and Gathering Information."* Since we've described the Goal of our story as *"revolving around a sensitive and dangerous piece of information,"* we choose *Gathering Information,* which is defined as learning.

- For *OS Outcome*, we choose *Failure* to give our story a tragic ending that stresses the required philosophical angle of the story.

- For *OS Driver,* we choose *Decisions Drive Actions* to make the crisis of the story a matter of Decision—perhaps a political decision that affects the life of others.

- For *OS Limit*, we choose *Optionlock* to limit the character's choices and thus force him to make the crisis decision.

- Here follows a tough choice: The *Subjective (Main Vs. Impact) Story Issue.* Of four possible choices, there are two that make an interesting story: *Permission (what is allowed)* which applies to our Main Character who's not allowed to tell he's a spy, or *Need (that which is required)* which applies to our Impact Character, a needy and deprived Russian. We still don't know enough about our story to make this choice, so we choose both. This forwards both terms to the space on the right, and postpones our final decision until later.

- This leaves eight possibilities for the final Storyforming question: *The Main Character's Problem.* After reviewing each of our possibilities several times, we choose *Protection.* Protection reflects the dual problems of the Secret Agent protecting his identity and the interests of his government.

The software tells us, *"Congratulations, you've arrived at one Storyform!"* That's great news, but do we know enough about our story to start illustrating the choices we've made?

It's time to review all we've done and let our imagination free, catching any idea that flows from our previous work. This is a good point to review the story's requirements, to see if we've forgotten to include anything, and finally, to start picturing our movie—to synthesize concrete ideas from the abstract ideas we've entered into our Storyform so far. The way to do this is to:

- Review all our answers.

- Ask why we chose each of the items.

- If there is an image that's suggested by it, jot it down.

We take a moment to synthesize all we've developed so far into a single idea. We try to fuse all that we've created while answering the previous questions and thus form a central concept that will direct our story.

After pondering on the previous work for a couple of hours, this is what I came up with:

> *"Set loosely against the catastrophe of the Nuclear Submarine Kursk, this movie is about Nick, an American spy in post-communist Russia, who knows about the faults in the submarine's construction. Nick wants to warn the local authorities to avoid a tragedy. However, his position as a secret agent and his own government policies forbid him from doing so."*

Good enough. We write this down in the *Plot Synopsis* screen that we previously left empty.

Also, with this idea, we can create the rest of our cast including our *Impact Character*. Here's my proposed IC:

> *"Marina (28 years old), an attractive Russian widow whose husband was killed in a previous submarine accident."*

Now, the genre tells us that in most **Spy films** the Impact Character has a villainous nature. So, Marina will be in direct opposition of Nick. Perhaps she'll work in counterespionage, or perhaps she'll just hate Americans because the accident that killed her husband was blamed on American sabotage by the Russian media. That should emphasize the Genre, but dramatic situations are called for also, so Marina's villainous nature won't be static. She may begin as an unsurpassable opposition, but later she'll be revealed as accepting guide, still later as an ally, and finally as a romantic interest. For now let's just keep this in mind. We'll have plenty of time to develop her thoroughly later.

Storyencoding

It's time to start *Storyencoding (illustrating)* our treatment. This is the time to write down what we've done so far. Let's put into words the ideas we formed while defining the logline and making choices for the storyform. Many of the Storyencoding items we already know (like the *MC Domain: "Nick is an American agent working undercover in a hostile country"*), while others we have to invent. For this creative work we rely on our *Logline*, on the help from the *Definition, Context,* and *Stories* buttons of the software, and on our good-old-pure imagination.

The key to Storyencoding is to ponder each question until we find an idea that has dramatic potential and stirs that "I can see this in a movie" feeling in us. The idea is to answer each question with material that can be later developed into a scene or a significant event. For example, which scene can arise out of *"Nick is an American Agent working undercover in a hostile country"*? How about *a scene where we see Nick posing as a convincing computer expert in Moscow, extracting data from a computer in an old military building, and later delivering that data in a mysterious envelope at the American Embassy?* Let's think over each question until something inspiring or interesting emerges and make mental notes of how it could be later developed into cinematic material.

Let's give it a try and illustrate some story points:

- *MC Domain of Situation.* As we already said, *"Nick is an American Agent working undercover in post-communist Russia."*

- *MC Concern of The Present.* We'll have to think this one over. Hmmm...

"At the present, after the end of the cold war, the current situation is a crisis in the intelligence agencies. They don't know what to do with their agents. They keep them in place, but they're ineffective as operatives."

- *MC Problem of Protection.* We already know this one, *"Nick has to protect his identity."*

- *MC Approach of a Do-er.* Let's think this one over. How about this, *"Nick is never satisfied with his bureaucratic work of merely delivering reports. His nature tells him to find solutions to the problems he's reporting and to put them into practice."*

- *MC's Mental Sex of Female (Intuitive Problem-Solving Style).* Let's look at the "Definition" and "Context" screens and think about this for a while. *"Nick always strives for justice. He goes for the fairest solution for each problem."*

- *MC Resolve of Change.* We already had a vague idea for this, so let's make it precise. *"Nick quits his job as a secret agent."*

- *MC Judgment Good.* Let's do the same here. *"Nick feels relieved by finally being able to tell the truth."*

- Next is a *Main Character Recap.* Let's skip it to keep the creative momentum and advance to the next questions:

- *OS Backstory*—This would be a good place to enter some brief research about the Kursk tragedy and the situation in Russia after the communist regime. So, make a note here saying that we have to research those items in the next few days, and let's go to the next question.

- *OS Domain of Activities*—Let's think about this one a bit and find some interesting material. Okay. *"Everyone in Russia is into erratic activities trying to find a place after the fall of the communism. Ex-party members try to open a business they don't know anything about. Ex-military men try to get into the Russian Mafia. Ex-secret agents try to sell their knowledge to whoever wants to buy it..."*

- *OS Goal of Gathering Information*—With all that we've developed so far this one won't be hard to invent. *"Nick learns about the design flaws in the submarines and wants to tell people before a tragedy occurs."*

- *OS Driver of Decisions*—Let's create at least two illustrations for this: one that starts the story and one that ends it. *"Nick is assigned as an inoperative spy in Russia because of the Intelligence Agency's lack of Decision"* and *"Nick decides to reveal the secret about the submarine dangers when it's too late."*

- *OS Limit of Optionlock*—The key here is to start thinking of options that will force the climax when exhausted. *"Nick tries to convince his government that averting the tragedy is more important than keeping the agency's secrecy. When this fails, Nick tries to filter the information without revealing his condition as a secret agent. Finally, Nick has no other alternative than to reveal he's a secret agent and risk being caught for spying to avoid a tragedy."*

- *OS Outcome of Failure*—Let's think of the last scenes of our story. *"Because of the political implications, the Russian government dismisses Nick's revelations and fails to avoid the tragedy."*

- Next comes a *Plot Synopsis Recap*. Let's use it just to check how much our answers resemble our early idea and how they've advanced it. Now let's go on.

- *SS Backstory*—This question is not essential to the story's development at this particular moment. So let's leave it blank and come back later.

- *SS Domain of Manipulation* —This question, on the other hand, is absolutely crucial at this particular moment, so let's think about it carefully and answer it the best we can. *"Nick builds an intricate maze of lies to convince Marina he's not a secret agent, then has to tear it down to show her the truth."*

- *SS Concern of Conceiving An Idea*—Another tricky question, let's ponder this one thoroughly. *"Nick thinks of a way to reveal the submarine dangers while saving his identity. This idea involves using Marina to channel the risky info, thus putting her at risk."*

- *SS Issue of Need*—We already knew something about this, let's expand on it. *"Marina has several obvious needs: she's impoverished, lonely, and in danger. Nick feels compelled to help her."*

Let's go on to the *Impact Character section:*

- *IC Domain of Fixed Attitude*—We already know this one. *"Marina firmly believes in the idealistic views of Communism."*

- *IC Concern of Contemplation*—This we have to create. *"Marina considers Nick's incongruent behavior, and before long she deduces he's a secret agent."*

- *IC Resolve of Steadfast*—The key to illustrating this is to realize that the steadfast character is an evolving character. She has an arc and progresses like every character. But a particular element of her personality remains consistent and grows in importance to the point of changing the MC. What could be this central element, this crucial characteristic in Marina's psyche, that changes Nick? *"Marina's supreme need for truth remains throughout her life."* That should do it.

After a few Recap questions—which we leave unaltered for now—this finishes the Storyforming part of the StoryGuide.

Cool.

We now have to tell all we've developed in the form of a story to weave it. Some ideas for scenes have already appeared. Some others are still in a sketchy stage and need to be developed.

This is okay. We still have thirteen days to turn all this stuff into a treatment.

What's important is that we've started the StoryGuide process with a few feeble ideas and ended up with a strong synopsis. We have a whole vision of our central characters, a general view of our plot, and a complete Storyform that will be the backbone of the entire project.

For now, let's just weave together all the material we've developed into a treatment. We start it with the scene where Nick extracts data from the military computer, or perhaps with the scene where he is deactivated as a spy. From there we can go to the scene where he learns about the flaws in the submarine, or perhaps the scene where he first meets Marina and their opposition starts. Continue to scenes where he makes plans to release the secure information, to his falling in love with her, and to his eventual decision to tell the secret. Wrap up the story with scenes of his danger of being captured for spying and his resigning from the agency.

There's a lot to tell here. We don't have to worry—we've developed plenty of material.

When the first treatment is sold and you have signed the contract for the screenplay's first draft, Dramatica will help you in writing it. Let's see how that's done in the next chapter.

12

NOTE AND SKETCH DEVELOPMENT

Muses never tell a story from beginning to end, do they?

No, most times they just whisper a situation or a scene description that immediately strikes us as an excellent idea for a movie. This inspires a couple of characters, a handful of scenes, and perhaps, a title. From there, the inspiration flow stops abruptly, and the Muses leave the writer alone to finish the story by himself with half a dozen unrelated items.

Darned Muses!

That's why we have structures—dramatic blueprints that allow us to develop those unrelated items, those scattered bits of inspiration into a complete story. Yep, structures are a creative blessing. The trick is to find the right one for our particular story. Do that and we're home free.

But how do we choose that right structure? Heck, Dramatica gives us no less than 32,768 to choose from. How do we know which one will work for us?

Good question. The answer is usually in the *Story Points* screen in Dramatica® Pro. Let's see how it's done.

Suppose you're in the following scenario:

> You're co-writing a ***Sci-Fi/Adventure/Dark Comedy*** about *a guy who travels to the future to find out that Reality-TV has replaced... well, reality.* In this project *the time-traveler arrives in a future world where every human appears in one or another of the three Reality-Shows on TV. Everyone dedicates his whole life to the tasks imposed by these programs, and only interrupts these activities to watch the other shows that involve the rest of humanity. Our hero learns that programs have replaced the Countries and Continents. The Americas have turned into a huge contest of tribes competing to survive in the wild. Australia and Asia's entire population compete in a singing competition. People all over Europe and Africa are locked inside their homes, voting each week to expel a member from their respective families. Wars have been replaced by rating points. The most watched show has complete control of the world. Cameras everywhere record every single act of every person, and the few*

*moments away from the contest is when they watch their own shows or
any of the other Reality-Shows of this brave new world on TV.*

You're planning to pitch it as "TRUMAN SHOW meets PLANET OF THE APES."
With your writing partner you've developed the synopsis, and have arrived at
the following premise: *"Crave For Fame Leads To Dehumanization."* You also have
these four scenes:

- *A scene, at some point at the beginning of the film, where the hero arrives
  in what looks like a savage, primitive world that, it turns out, is just the
  location of the surviving-tribes-reality-show.*

- *Another scene about an international summit where the world leaders—
  the shows' producers and executives—scrutinize the ratings and propose
  extreme measures (such as switching 'vote-outs' for executions) to
  improve the viewing percentages.*

- *Another scene where the hero falls in love with a young woman and
  she falls in love with him, but she cannot understand sexual intimacy
  without a camera recording them.*

- *A final, surprise ending scene where the hero frees the world population
  from the oppression imposed by the Reality-Shows, but the people he has
  just freed condemn him because he's robbing them of their chance for
  fame.*

And... that's all you've developed so far.

Let's add to this scenario that your alleged co-writer is a passionate guy who
has fallen in love with every one of the above-described scenes. He fervently adores
the premise and is obsessed with the situation. He won't allow the slightest change
in the original material, but he leaves the further development of the story to his
partner. It is up to you to turn all this into a story.

How will you turn this bunch of inspiration sparks, this handful of dramatic
wishes, into a finished script? How will you transform it into a decent movie that will
entertain audiences everywhere?

Time to go to the Dramatica software, of course.

To introduce notes and sketches from previously written material into
Dramatica, and to find the right Storyform for a partially developed story, we start
with the obvious and work to the more vague. We begin our storyform by entering
the more clearly defined items. That gives us the path to identify the obscure ones.

Say, we already have a more or less clear definition on the Genre: *Sci-Fi/
Adventure/Dark Comedy*. Now, *Sci-Fi* and *Adventure* films usually use an *OS
Domain of Activities*, so we can set this in the Story Engine to start our Storyform.

We also have a premise: *"Crave For Fame Leads To Dehumanization."* A quick analysis (like we did on the "Storyforming From A Premise" chapter) gives us the following items:

- *"Crave"* gives us an MC *Growth* of *Stop.*

- *"For Fame"* gives us an OS *Issue* of *Self-Interest.*

- *"Leads To Dehumanization"* gives us a *Story Judgment* of *Bad.*

These choices have trimmed down our search for the perfect structure and, more importantly, have made sure that our Genre and Premise are firmly imbedded into our story.

Let's work with the rest of our material. Since we're stepping now out of the obvious and into obscure matters, we'll have to continue in a different way.

The first step is to break this material into "story bits," to separate each idea of what we've written, and round each of them into independent ideas. Take this paragraph from the brief synopsis:

> *"The time-traveler arrives in a future world where every human appears in one or another of the three Reality-Shows on TV. Everyone dedicates their lives to the tasks imposed by this program, and only interrupts these daily activities to watch the other shows that involve the rest of humanity."*

This paragraph can be divided into the following four "bits," into these four independent ideas:

- *"The time-traveler arrives in a future world."*

- *"Every human appears in one or another of the three Reality-Shows on TV."*

- *"Everyone dedicates their lives to the tasks imposed by this program."*

- *"(Everybody) only interrupts (the contest) daily activities to watch the other shows that involve the rest of humanity."*

With this completed, let's open the Story Points screen in the Dramatica software. This lists all the important points of a story in a table format. It has a column for:

- The Story Points (Appreciations)—*The function a particular point has in a story*

- The Items—*The nature of that particular point*

- The Definitions—*A description of how the particular point's nature works in that particular function in the story*

- It also includes *Storytelling space* to jot down our developed points.

Story Point	Item	Definition	Illustrations
Genre Points			
Dynamics			
Resolve		the ultimate disposition of the Main Character to Change or Remain Steadfast	
Growth	Stop	regarding the Main Character, the audience is waiting for something to end	
Approach	Do-er	the Main Character looks for a physical solution to her problem	

Some Items are chosen and some remain to be decided, but for now, let's insert our previously developed ideas, all the little paragraphs we've just made into the Storytelling spaces.

Let's start with this one: *"The time-traveler arrives in a future world."* Where shall it go? We have to realize that any paragraph can go into several places and that any idea can satisfy many different story needs. *"The time-traveler arrives in a future world"* can be used as *MC Domain* because it describes our hero as a fish out of water—the condition that defines him throughout the story. It can be used as the *Story Driver*, because this arrival sets the story in motion. Or it can be used as a *Signpost 1* for any throughline—any thread can explore the sources and effects of this arrival in the first act of the story.

Which is the real function for this idea? Where is the perfect place in the structure for it? The short answer is this: there isn't a perfect place. It's all an aesthetic decision; it's all *our* aesthetic decision. The paragraph could go anywhere, represent any function, and—as long as it goes into one story point and its storyform item represents it accurately—it will stand coherently and properly within the rest of the story. That's the beauty of the storyform and the story points system. We can stick any idea anywhere, choose the storyform accordingly, and the software will give us a coherent story every time.

Story Point	Item	Definition	Illustrations
Driver	Action	in terms of the Overall plot, actions force decisions	The time-traveler arrives in a future world.

Let's suppose we insert *"The time-traveler arrives in a future world"* as the *Story Driver*, and then go to the Story Engine window to choose a Driver of *Action*. This shortens our trip to the perfect structure by half.

Now, let's do one a little bit trickier:

> *"Every human appears in one or another of the three Reality-Shows on TV."*

We first ask ourselves if this paragraph is a *Genre Point* (defining the style of story we're writing), a *Thematic Point* (defining its meaning), or a *Plot Point* (altering its development course). Where would we like it to go? What would make more sense to us? This too is an aesthetic decision, so we'll take a moment to consider the paragraph fully and decide. Let's use it as a *Thematic Point*.

Let's go to the Story Points window, find the Thematic Points section and see how they're organized. Here we have to ask ourselves if the paragraph is part of the *Overall Story throughline* (affects all the characters), or the *Main Character throughline* (affects the hero). Or is it part of the *Impact Character throughline* (affects the character that makes the deepest influence on the hero), or the *Subjective (Main vs. Impact) Story throughline* (affects the relationship between the two more significant characters)? The paragraph itself gives us the answer to this question (*"...every human appears..."*), so we use it as part of the *Overall Story*.

Now comes the hardest question for this paragraph. We have to choose if it makes more sense as the *OS Domain, Concern, Issue, Counterpoint, Thematic Conflict, Problem, Solution, Symptom, Response, Benchmark, Catalyst, or Inhibitor.* The "Definition" column in the Story Points table helps us in finding this paragraph's place, but more significant help can be found in the "Item" column, because some of the items are already storyformed. Reading those items, their definitions, and the definitions of the rest of the Story Points, gives us an idea where to put the paragraph, *"Every human appears in one or another of the three Reality-Shows on TV"*? For me, it makes sense as the *OS Concern of Obtaining*. It shows both the contestants' ambition to win the prize and the humanity's feeling of imprisonment, of captivity in this world of eternal contest shows.

Edit Illustration

Illustrate how the area of shared concern in the Overall Story (Concern) concerns achieving or possessing something (**Obtaining**):

Every human appears in one or another of the three Reality-Shows on TV.

Okay, so we open the "Edit Illustration" (or "Edit Storytelling") space on the *OS Concern* cell of the table and insert, *"Every human appears in one or another of the three Reality-Shows on TV"* as the *OS Concern of Obtaining*.

Let's do a couple more paragraphs.

> *"Everyone dedicates their entire lives to the tasks imposed by this program."* This sounds to me like another *Theme Point* belonging to the *Overall Story throughline*. It seems to show the active nature of the *OS Domain of Activities*.

> *"(Everybody) only interrupts (the contest) daily activities to watch the other shows that involve the rest of humanity."* This is yet another *Theme Point*, but I can't match it to any of the present items of the Overall Story. So I run through the rest of the Theme Points Items in the Story Point table and find *"A Fixed Attitude Or Outlook."* This describes the sense of everyone obsessing every single moment of their lives over the programs, but it's listed as the *Impact Character's Domain*. Not to worry, we inscribe the paragraph as *Impact Character's Domain of Fixed Attitude* with a slight wording change to describe this appreciation more accurately:

> *"The Impact Character (just like everybody else) only interrupts the contest activities to watch the daily shows involving the rest of this obsessed humanity."*

Using this paragraph as the IC Domain has the advantage that it already starts telling us about our Impact Character. We explore a new thread and advance the general concept of our story. As I've pointed out earlier, the point where we place each paragraph is an aesthetic choice. We must choose wisely and always try to advance our script's development.

Now, let me pause a moment to say a thing or two about inserting our scenes. Usually, 'scenes' mean Plot Points. They define turning points in the story and describe the beginning, middle and end, so we look mostly in the Plot Points Section of the Story Points table to find their proper place. For example, our final "surprise ending" scene (*"The hero frees the world population from the oppression of the imposed Reality-Shows, but the people he has just freed condemn him because he's robbing them of their chance for fame"*) could imply an *Outcome* of *Success* (*"The hero frees the world population from the oppression of the imposed Reality-Shows"*). It may also imply a *Judgment* of *Bad* (*"The people he has just freed condemn him because he's robbing them of their chance for fame"*). So this scene may be used to describe two important Plot Points in our Storyform.

Many times, scenes go in as *Signposts*, as points to pass in the story's development, rather than permanent Plot defining items. Our first scene may go in easily as *Signpost 1 of The Past.*

- First Scene: *"The hero arrives in what looks like a savage, primitive world that turns out to be just the location of the surviving-tribes-reality-show."*

- Signpost 1 of The Past Scene: *A scene where our hero thinks he has traveled to the past instead of the future, and later discovers the future is a commercial parody of the prehistoric days.*

Since the *MC Throughline* is the one with the *Situation Domain*, we can write this scene in the Edit Illustration space for the *MC Signpost 1*. Then, go to the *Plot Progression Screen* and set the storyform for *MC Signpost 1* to *"The Past."*

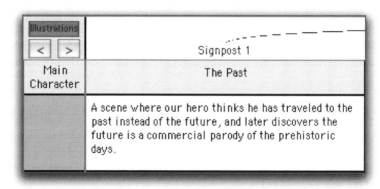

That's the general idea of how to develop our story fully from some early material by using the Story Points table. Take our notes and sketches. Divide them into individual ideas. Give each idea a place in the structure by choosing Storyform items along the way and adapting the wording to make the paragraph fit while keeping the original idea.

Completing a Storyform and finishing the story in the Story Points table is a piece of cake. We can identify all our missing points at a glance. Creating them follows naturally by using the knowledge gained during the analysis and identification of the original material. This is a fun and productive process.

Another good use of the Story Points table is in the rewriting stages. We can keep all the material we love and fancy, yet change the structure to gain a different effect on our story. Want a happier ending? A Success/Good finale will brighten this dark comedy. We don't have to scratch out the scene where the hero is condemned, just change it to another place and give it another function. The material remains—

it is the structure that changes. And the structure adapts to whatever story we want to create with our cherished material.

Speaking of rewriting stages, let's see what Dramatica has to offer for these final phases of the development process and for fully finishing a complete draft.

13

THOROUGH DEVELOPMENT

Tailors have this saying about making suits, "It is easier to make a piece from scratch than to fix one that's already made."

I don't know if that's true in tailoring, but it sure is true for writing.

The rewriting process and the final stages of thorough development of a rough draft are the trickiest parts of completing a screenplay. These are the steps when we can make a good story superb, or ruin it all and turn it into incomprehensible garbage. Many writers freak out at this point and instead of rewriting, throw away everything and write a whole new story, keeping just the characters' names and a couple of events they liked.

But there's no need to do that, nor is it always possible.

Imagine this scenario:

A producer who knows you and trusts in you calls one day and says, "We're working on a **Mystery/Psycho Thriller/Drama** project, and the script is 'almost there,' but still lacks...uh, it needs more 'mystery,' more twists and turns, more surprises. There are still a few plot holes, the characters could use a little extra motivation, and the first act drags a bit while the third act is somewhat hasty and confusing. Anyway, I was wondering if you could handle the rewrites, do some fine-tuning, take a few bugs out of it. You will? Great, my assistant will bring you a copy this afternoon—no, make that in an hour."

And the assistant comes by, brings you the script and you start reading it right away.

> *"It starts with Katherine, a middle-aged woman who's rushed into a hospital with a severe case of intoxication. She arrives at the brink of death, but the doctors manage to save her. Several scenes follow with the doctors trying to find the cause of intoxication. It turns out it's a rare and lethal poisonous agent. Here follows a lengthy investigation to find out how she could ever get in contact with this toxin. At the end of Act I, William, Katherine's husband, declares that she took it intentionally, and then he painfully reveals that his wife has suffered secretly and long from a severe mental illness. This has led to acute delusional paranoia and to her suicide attempt.*

"In the Second Act, Mia, an intern at the psychiatry ward in the hospital, takes an interest in Katherine's case. She puts Katherine through some tests and discovers the patient doesn't have the profile of a paranoid. Mia tells her discoveries to the other doctors, but they dismiss her. She then asks William for proof of Katherine's illness. He can't produce any medical evidence, but tells Mia that his wife has gone to the extent of believing he wants to murder her. Mia keeps digging and discovers a long and bitter history of William's infidelity. At some point he was planning to divorce Katherine to marry his lover, but he was unable to give up Katherine's wealth, so he kept his adultery a secret. Mia also finds out that William has free access to the poisonous agent that almost killed his wife. Parallel to these discoveries are three hidden attempts to murder Katherine throughout the second act. An attempt to kill Mia closes this act.

"In act III, Mia plans to alert the police about the discoveries, but yet another murder attempt makes her realize that William is aware of the findings. Somehow, she assumes the only way to stop William is by confronting him before he can destroy the evidence, so she goes to face him alone. On seeing Mia, William feels immediately threatened, and without giving her any time to explain, he attacks her. William chases Mia to the rooftop of a tall building where he corners her. Mia defends herself and William falls to his death. The police arrive, Mia tells her story and they consider William as guilty and immediately close the case. Mia goes to the hospital to tell Katherine the bad news, but Katherine cynically confesses that this was all her plan, a ploy to punish her cheating husband."

Okay—you realize—"take a few bugs out of it" was an understatement.

So rewrites are in order, but where should you begin the rewrites? How could you imbed this with more 'mystery,' upgrade it with more surprises? How could you fix the plot holes, bring out the characters' motivation, strengthen the narrative drive?

Don't panic, there's no need to throw it all away and start all over. Here's how Dramatica can help in restructuring and improving the example draft.

Let's begin by opening the software and going directly to the *"Query System"* screen. We're going to need two files for this: A file for the original version and another for the rewrite. First we need an analysis of the original. Let's open the *"Storyforming—Complete"* screen.

Now, we need to reread the script and take notes of the structure items that are obvious. We need to have in mind all that we know about Dramatica and try to find in the script any points that direct us to its structure.

Let's say, for starters, that it's obvious that *Actions Drive the Story* in this story: *Katherine arrives at the hospital, William reveals she has mental illness, the investigations, the murder attempts...*all actions. So we go to the *Story Driver* screen in the *Plot Dynamics* section and check *"Actions Drive Decisions"* to begin our structure.

It's also clear the story has an *Outcome of Success* since Mia gets to the bottom of the mystery, but a *Judgment of Bad* since in the process, the innocent was killed and the true culprit went unpunished. So we're going to check *Success as the Outcome* and *Bad as the Judgment* in their respective screens in the Plot Dynamics section.

From here we have to decide on some less obvious structure items, such as, who are the Central Characters in this story? According to *Genre*, Mia should be the *Main Character*, and William should be the *Impact Character.* In a **Mystery**, the crime solver is the Main Character and the false clue and an *uncertain person* represents the Impact Character. We'll have to move Mia's introduction earlier in the story because she is presented way too late in the script.

Fine, that will do. Now we have to develop them.

In the script, Mia never stops in her effort to solve the mystery; she is a *Steadfast Main Character.* So we go to the *Character Dynamics* section and check *Steadfast* as the *Main Character Resolve.* Also, Mia clearly is a *Do-er* since she deals with the problem externally by investigating and confronting, instead of internally adapting. We'll mark *Do-er* as the character's *Approach.*

What else is there? Well, that's all we know about the characters' dynamics from the script. From here we have to select the structure's *Throughlines* and their *Story Points*, but the screenplay is even less clear about them. Let's try to mark whatever we can find.

There seems to be an *Overall Story Domain of Activities*—since all that happens in the story are activities—so we enter that into the *OS Story Points* section. In addition, there's an apparent *Overall Story Concern of Gathering Information*—since all the activities are about gathering information: Examining the toxic substance, testing Katherine's mental condition, and looking into William's infidelities. We enter that one too.

The draft doesn't have much more information about the structure and it leaves us with an incomplete Storyform. This is common in first drafts, and that's a reason they hired us to rewrite it. So, we're done with the Storyform of this file. We close the *Storyforming—Complete* screen, open the *Storytelling—Complete* topic list, and we continue to fill in the spaces of the chosen Appreciations with the events and ideas of the first draft. We make sure to use the bits of information that made us choose these appreciations:

- Under *Resolve: Steadfast* in the *Character Dynamics section*, we write, *"Mia never stops in her effort to solve the mystery."*

- Under *Approach: Do-er* in the *Character Dynamics section*, we write *"Mia deals with the problem externally by investigating and confronting."*

- Under *Driver: Action* in the *Plot Dynamics section*, we list the activities that drive the acts: *"Katherine arrives at the hospital; William reveals his wife's mental condition; Mia runs tests on Katherine; there are three attempts on Katherine's life..."*

Do the same with every one of our chosen appreciations. We need to enter all the useful information of the first draft to use it productively in the rewrite.

When this is done, save the file under the name *"draft-1"* (or whatever name you choose to identify this draft), then save it again (with the command *"Save As..."*) under the new name *"draft-2."* This new file is the one we're going to use to rework the story.

Let the rewrites begin.

In our analysis of the first version we've noticed the Storyform is incomplete, so we first have to get a full Storyform. Let's open the *Storyforming—Complete* screen in the Query System to choose the omitted appreciations:

- We choose *"Female (Intuitive)"* as the *Main Character's Mental Sex (Problem-Solving Style)* to give Mia the intuition to investigate the case and by sympathizing fall into Katherine's trap.

- We choose *"Optionlock"* as the *Story Limit* to let the characters run out of options and force them to face the killer in order to survive.

Our Storyform is starting to get a fuller, better structure, but now we may have to consider changing some items of the first Storyform to improve it even more. For example:

- The *OS Domain of Activities* doesn't help much for highlighting the **Mystery** Genre; an *OS Domain of Manipulations* is much better for manipulating the audience and thus creating surprises and unexpected twists.

- The *OS Concern of Gathering Information* should also change: A new *OS Concern of Developing a Plan* gives the story's Central Concern (picturing what happened the night that Katherine took the poison) more clarity and emphasis.

With these two items changed, we go directly to finish our Storyform:

- Let's choose the *OS Problem*. The screen gives us sixteen different elements from which to choose. We consider each one carefully, read their *Definitions* and *Context* examples, and even try a few before deciding on one. After all this, we choose *Perception* (the way things seem to be) to underline a story troubled by appearances.

And there we have it, a complete Storyform. Congratulations are in order.

With a complete Storyform—a full structure—it's possible to produce a rewrite that is a well-considered, more interesting story while saving the original events and ideas of the first draft. We can build up from what we've already worked to reach another plateau, an upper state of story that has better characters, a more sound plot, plus more brilliant and more thrilling genre elements.

We'll build this second draft on a "What If...?" basis. Instead of concocting new material, we let the Storyform Story Points inspire new perspectives that will improve the original material. We let the story point ask "What If...?" to what has already been written.

For example:

> Mia, the Main Character, has a *Situation* Domain, a Concern of the *Past*, and a Problem of *Thought*. This means that Mia lives in a special external condition that's centered on her history and causes troubles in her process of consideration. Now, let's release our imagination and ask "What if...?" What could be the external condition centered on Mia's history that troubles her process of consideration? Hmmmm, we should think about this for a while, try different alternatives and always try to go further, always try to arrive at a new level that would make the story more interesting, more original. Hmm, let's say:

> *"What if Mia had a history of psychosis in her family? What if her mother went insane and died in an asylum and Mia is now worried about inheriting it? What if she's afraid she'll suddenly develop that mental disease and start thinking erratically, start becoming mad?"*

Okay, Mia starts becoming more interesting than the mere hospital-intern/crime-solver that she was before. Let's try developing another character.

William, the Impact Character, has a Domain of *Fixed Attitude*, a Concern of *Memory*, and a Problem of *Perception*. This means that William makes his biggest Impact with a fixed idea based on recollections that are driven by the way things seem to be. Hmm...

"What if William was a famous psychiatrist, in fact one of Mia's professors in medical school? What if William made a deep impact on her? What if she remembers him as the perfect doctor, a caring and wise physician, her professional role model and perhaps a father-like figure?"

So, William (Dr. William, if you please) starts getting more involved in the story. He's no longer a character that only served as an obvious red herring. Now, how about the crime-solving thread? Where shall we put it?

The Subjective Story has an *Activities* Domain, a Concern of *Understanding*, and a Problem of *Inequity*. This means that Mia and William are bonded by activities that are aimed to appreciate the meaning of something, and are upset by a dilemma of unfairness. Fine, say, I have an idea—what if this was the Crime-Solving thread?

"What if Mia researches Katherine's poisoning, but can't understand the clues since all evidence leads to William as the prime suspect, and she thinks this is unfair?"

Twists and turns are beginning to appear in the initially flat first draft. Let's see what new perspectives this modest work inspires:

- Mia may take a sudden plunge into madness, and then she may recover and find that her seeming madness was in fact telling her the final truth.

- William may appear first as a perfect doctor and teacher, then as a troubled husband, then as a devious killer and finally as a victim of his wife's plots.

- The Subjective Story—their relationship—will be a thread of sweet lies and bitter discoveries, of deceptions and disillusions, preconceptions, and shocks.

Can we go further with the twists and turns? Let's see:

The Overall Story has a *Manipulation Domain*, a *Concern of Developing a Plan*, and a Problem of *Perception*. This means that all the characters have peculiar ways of thinking, try to envision something, and are troubled by the way things seem to be. Now, "what if...?" Okay, let's go for broke here. Let's think several possibilities for this thread, then choose the most original, and then ponder it more to expand it even further. Hmm...

"What if all the characters are either mental patients or students of psychiatry? What if they are part of an experiment to envisage madness, to understand the mind of the mentally ill, and to break the conventions of psychosis classifications?" There. This should surround our story in a delusive environment, a situation where neither the characters nor the audience is sure of what's real and what's not. A story where surprises and plot twists emerge naturally, and the "mystery" and "psycho thriller" flourish.

Where can we go from here? Anywhere. The Storytelling part of rewriting is a process of endless change. The new storyform story points inspire deeper, more interesting perspectives, and these perspectives in turn make the original ideas and events deeper and more interesting. Every new story item inspires the next, and little-by-little, step-by-step, it all starts making sense. The new draft starts appearing right before our eyes, and we have finally imbedded this with more *mystery*, upgraded it with surprises, fixed the plot holes, brought out the characters' motivation, and strengthened the narrative drive.

Let's see a brief example of how this chaotic-yet-creative, unruly-yet-prolific process of writing in the Query System inspires one idea after another:

- *The Overall Story Throughline* is now a thread about *"an unconventional experiment to envisage how a psychotic mind thinks."* This inspires:

- *The Overall Story Signpost 1: Developing a Plan,* which is now a scene where *"William—head of psychiatry at the hospital and researcher in charge of the unconventional experiment—explains his plans for the investigation. It involves a drug that induces brief delusional states, and is harmless if taken in small doses, but lethal if overdosed."* This scene arises:

- *The Story Driver: Action,* which is still when *"Katherine arrives at the hospital with a severe intoxication."* But now, *"the poison turns out to be an overdose of the drug her husband was using in the experiment."* This event leads us to create:

- *The Story Consequence: Understanding*—Here *"the doctors manage to save Katherine, but the drug has left her confused. She utters a disjointed description of how and why she took the drug, but nobody is able to understand her."* This point takes us to:

- *The Story Goal: Developing a Plan,* where *"the doctors, the police and Mia strive to imagine what happened the night Katherine took the poison."* We may choose to use the cinematic technique of a recurring flashback scene, one that changes slightly every time a new fact is discovered until completing the truth. This directs us to produce:

- *The Story Requirement: Conceiving an Idea,* which is about how *"all the clues point toward William as the culprit in Katherine's poisoning, but Mia cannot imagine her perfect teacher perpetrating that hideous crime."* From here we jump to:

- *The Overall Story Signpost 2: Playing a Role,* a scene where *"Mia abruptly begins to suffer from hallucinations and acute anxiety attacks. She temporarily lives a life of madness and wonders if she accidentally has taken the drug."* This moves us to:

- *The Story Forewarnings: The Present,* where *"Mia realizes that she has been intentionally poisoned like Katherine, that she escaped death or permanent brain damage by a hair, and that her life is in danger."* From here we step to:

- *The Overall Story Signpost 3: Changing One's Nature,* a scene where *"Mia's hallucinations become more and more recurrent and bizarre. She wonders now if she has become psychotic like her mother or if it's only a temporary state produced by the drug."* This moves us to:

- *The Story Limit: Optionlock,* where *"Mia realizes this is her last chance to identify the cause of her delusions. She must confront William and force him to admit or refute responsibility for her poisoning."*

You get the idea.

Working within this new, improved storyform, illustrating it creatively, then weaving it carefully and giving it some narrative drive, our new draft of the story may become this:

> *The story starts with Katherine, a modest, middle-aged woman, wandering aimlessly through the streets of a high-class shopping district. She enters an expensive shop and, without provocation, begins thrashing the merchandise on the shelves. The police arrive and she is forcibly restrained. Katherine babbles wildly*

*something about how her husband 'poisoned her mind' and how
'he poisoned the mind of all his students.' She is transferred to a
hospital where we meet Mia, an intern at the psychiatry ward in
the hospital. Mia examines Katherine, diagnoses her actions as an
'acute schizophrenic episode,' and asks for Katherine's documents to
notify her relatives. On seeing her last name Mia gasps. Katherine's
husband, Dr. William Yolesi, is one of Mia's favorite medical school
instructors.*

*At this point we are introduced to William. We learn about his
unorthodox experiments designed to understand the psychotic mind.
We also learn about Mia's relationship with William—about the great
admiration she has for him. During a break in Katherine's testing,
Mia contacts her teacher about his wife. Mia asks if the drug used in
the research could have produced Katherine's episode. William finds
this assumption absurd. Mia follows William to the police precinct.
To clear his experiment of any implied connection with Katherine's
breakdown, William reveals Katherine's secret, long battle with
mental illness. He also tells the police about a loud argument he had
with his wife the previous night that likely contributed to his wife's
mental collapse.*

*As William relates all this, Mia privately recalls her own
family's history of struggle against psychosis. Mia tells him of
her schizophrenic mother, how this frustration led Mia to study
psychiatry, the help William gave her to understand her family's
disease and the latent fear of inheriting it that shadows Mia all the
time.*

*William finishes his statement, but the police don't buy it. They say
they can't rule out foul play yet and that they'll have to consider
William a suspect until they finish the investigation. Mia comes to
William's defense. Her anger at the police's distrust of William covers
her feelings of guilt for doubting her teacher. On leaving the precinct
she apologizes to William, but he rebuffs her. Using a patronizing
tone of voice, William makes a cruel remark about her qualms being
normal for someone with her background of mental health troubles.
Mia accepts this quietly and shivers at the possibility of succumbing
to her family's disease.*

The police ask for Katherine's lab tests. The tests come back positive for William's psychotropic drug. William is now the prime suspect in a criminal investigation, and his experiment is shut down. William admits the tests were always on the brink of getting out of hand. Some subjects experienced flashbacks or unexpectedly prolonged delusions that lasted days. But he declares that a mistake as big as someone outside the research taking the drug is not possible.

Mia also can't understand how this slip-up could have happened and surmises someone is framing her teacher. She decides to take some time to investigate what happened and how the drug ever got to Katherine. Here we get to know a little about Mia's life. She is a strict person, an order-freak that exorcised her mental demons through stern discipline and a tight schedule, but now her inquiries are turning her life upside down. Mia finds herself abandoning her internship more and more to spend time talking with the still recovering Katherine, trying to find clarification for what happened on the night before her incident.

Mia also volunteers to organize William's files to have a chance to talk with the subjects of the experiment. She finds out that most of them suffer long-term effects from the experimental drug. Some subjects were students who dropped out of medical school because of permanent damage. They are emotionally unstable and harbor feelings of resentment toward William. Mia feels she's alienating these unstable people, and in turn they wonder out loud why she is throwing away her future as a talented psychiatry student to become William's personal assistant. Rumors start about a romance between the two.

Mia tries to put the gossip out of her mind but, while organizing William's files, discovers that William has kept an adulterous relationship for some time. She confronts him and he confirms it. Mia finds out that Katherine discovered William's infidelity the night before her "incident" and threatened to kill herself. Mia is shocked, and William says he was never the 'perfect soul' she has so arbitrarily imagined him to be. He declares that he's a human being with flaws and weaknesses like everyone else. He ends this argument with a slight sign of violence—something that Mia would never have thought possible of him.

In the next few days, Mia feels uncomfortable when near her teacher. Her nervousness grows and grows until the she starts having minor hallucinations. She thinks she's poured herself a cup of coffee when the liquid isn't even brewed. She's certain of putting something in its place and then finding it in the oddest spot. Mia wonders if she has accidentally come in contact with William's drug, or if her disease is finally taking charge of her mind. She takes some blood tests, and the result for drug presence shows negative. Startled, she temporarily resigns from her internship, stops organizing William's files and takes a few days off to regain control of her thoughts. However, the hallucinations continue. They become more and more recurrent, bizarre and significant (she hears Katherine's voice coming out of her closet; on another night her dead mother sits in her living room and talks to her). Mia goes to the hospital lab to take another blood test, and the assistant tells her that she never took a first test. There's not a record of it at all. Mia wonders if she hallucinated the test or if someone has erased the evidence from the lab's files.

One day, Mia wakes up and finds her apartment wrecked. She can't recall it happening, but finds clues that leave no doubt she did it herself. Mia remembers her mother displayed similar behavior during the worst days of her illness and is now certain the experimental drug has nothing to do with her delusional states. She breaks down spiritually, convinced that her disease has taken complete control of her. After more than a few days of deep depression and uncanny visions, Mia gets enough courage to ask William for help, the one person she once identified as the source of mental health.

Mia gets to William's office, but finds he's not there. She looks for his address book to find his emergency phone number, and accidentally discovers the experimental drug in William's desk—where it shouldn't be. Mia examines the labeled brown glass, unable to understand how it got there. William arrives unexpectedly and violently seizes the container from her, pockets it and warns her against saying anything about finding the experimental drug in his office. Baffled, Mia stammers that she just came to ask for help. William says that he's through with her and her mental troubles. He makes some cruel remarks and asks her to leave—immediately.

Mia rushes away perplexed and tortured. She begins to realize that each truth she has discovered about William works to destroy her image of him as a perfect, kind teacher. She finally realizes that he could be poisoning Katherine, the clues obviously point to this fact, and that perhaps he has poisoned her as well. Mia goes to the police to tell them her deductions.

Mia talks to the police, but can't produce any hard evidence. They ask if she's sure she saw the drug in William's desk and whether she could testify in a court of law. Mia abruptly stops and confesses she's not sure. She discloses having recent hallucinations. She admits the possibility of having imagined the bottle in William's drawer as well the violent conversation that followed her discovery. When pushed, she is even unsure about all her previous discoveries. The police's attitude changes from interest to bored disappointment. They make an unconvincing promise that they'll investigate her claims against William. Mia returns home more frightened and confused than ever.

On arriving at her apartment, Mia finds William sitting in her living room. She tells him that she went to the police, and he tells her that he had expected it. Mia feels certain threat in William's tone and tries to get away, but the doctor holds her and blocks the door. He starts talking about his experiment, how he was expecting recognition and glory from it, and how it ruined his career instead. He explains the drug is safe, that he even tested it on himself just to show it was harmless to his students. William then tells Mia the last straw was her going to the police to accuse him of attempted murder. He bleakly laughs. He wonders aloud that perhaps he should kill her, and how easy it would be for him to create an alibi. 'An intern with a history of family psychosis tries to commit suicide. The concerned teacher tries to stop her, but arrives too late.' Saying this, William opens the window of Mia's eighth floor apartment. Mia fears that he is going to try to throw her out the window, but instead he mutters something about 'how thoughtless can a teacher be to do that?' and simply jumps to his death.

Mia calls 911 and sits down to wait.

After a few days, the police release Mia by finding no evidence that incriminates her. Mia is free, but feels guilty. She goes to the hospital to see Katherine, and the older woman immediately asks if William is dead yet. Mia asks her how she knew, and Katherine candidly confesses that she planned everything. She tells Mia what happened on the night before her lapse. Katherine got mad when she found out about her husband's infidelity, had a loud quarrel with him, and threatened to kill herself. She stayed up all night planning revenge. She knew that William's experiment was important to his career and that his life would be over if it failed. She explains that it was only a matter of getting hold of a little amount of the drug, taking it while in public, and waiting. She knew that one thing would lead to another. Shocked by this cynical revelation, Mia threatens to go to the police and tell them. Katherine scoffs, 'Poor child, who'd believe a crazy girl like you? You can't tell if you're hallucinating this conversation. You can't tell if you've just imagined my husband's death. In fact, you can't really tell which part of you're recent experience is truth and what is an invention of your diseased mind.'

Confused and frightened, Mia exits and starts wandering aimlessly through the streets.

There. I just love scary endings, don't you?

A note of interest. The idea of blurring the boundaries between Mia's hallucinations and what happens in "reality" and the "open ending" that results from it (where the Main Character—and therefore, the audience—can't tell exactly which is which) was implied by the Storyform. This is an example of how Dramatica can create an unconventional ending, heightening the genre and creating a very interesting piece.

Writing with the Query System is chaotic by nature. We skip from one story point to another with no more order than our muse tells us. Sometimes preliminary work with "*Dramatica in Thirty Seconds*" or "*Instant Dramatica*" is recommended to understand and imagine the structure of this second draft. Other times it is possible to create each story point by itself, just letting the imagination command the project, and jotting down whatever the story point suggests to us at the time. Don't worry—working within a Storyform assures us we'll end up with a perfectly coherent story.

And finally, the only rule for rewriting, the one commandment for thoroughly developing a story, is to :

ALWAYS MAKE NEW DRAFTS BETTER
THAN THE PREVIOUS DRAFTS

If some new material feels out of place, we should rethink it until we find its true place, or simply throw it away. If something new seems less exciting than the first version, we can always go back to the first version. "Rewriting" should be synonymous with "Enhancing," and that's our main objective.

So...

Let's say we've thoroughly developed our story. We've put surprises at the beginning and end of the story, shocks in every act, and twists and turns in each of the sixteen signposts. But we still need a lot more events to fill a two-hour movie with thrills and chills. Let's continue to see some ways to develop the plot and get all the twists that we could ever need for our story.

3 ACTS,
16 SEQUENCES
AND 48 SCENES

HOW TO GET
THE COMPLETE PLOT

14

ACT, SEQUENCE AND SCENE
AS PLOT TWISTS

Let's step away from Dramatica to ask a question so important for writers that most writers never get to ask it. What makes a Plot?

Better yet, what makes an *interesting* Plot?

Most screenwriting books will tell you, "A Plot is made by a succession of Events." But what makes an "Event"? Well, most books will tell you, "An Event is made of Dramatic Change." Then again, what makes "Dramatic Change?"

Books and creative writing teachers explain the term Event with examples such as the following:

> *"Suppose you park your car outside your office. You go in and work for four hours straight, and when you come out again, the car is wet. While you were inside working, an Event—in this case, rain—has taken place."*

Was the rain an Event? Well, I suppose it was. But it sure wasn't made of Dramatic Change.

Now, consider the following example:

> *"Suppose you park your car outside your office, and enter your intending to work for four hours straight, but a few minutes later you hear a runaway semi careening through the street. You run outside in time to see the semi crush your car into a pile of shapeless, corroded steel."*

Was that an event?

Heck, yeah!

Did it have Dramatic Change?

Absolutely.

A true Event—one made of one hundred percent pure Dramatic Change—has the following characteristics:

- *It's irreversible.*

- *It changes the characters' circumstances.*

- *It gives the characters new and more important purposes.*

- *It's meaningful to the characters (and, therefore, to the audience).*

"False" Events

Let's see how the "wet car" Event complies with these characteristics:

- *Is it irreversible?* No, a quick trip to the car wash will leave it as sparkling and dry as it ever was.

- *Does it change the characters' circumstances?* No, a little water won't make the car less serviceable or less valuable.

- *Does it give the characters new and more important purposes?* No, the character can go back to work for another four hours.

- *Is it meaningful to the characters?* Not at all—therefore, it is meaningless to the audience, and thus, a waste of time.

When we have an event that doesn't comply with any of these characteristics, it's what is known as a "false event."

"True" Events

On the other hand, let's see how the "totaled car" event stands against them:

- *Is it irreversible?* Yes, all the world's mechanics and all the world's car detailers can't put that car back together again.

- *Does it change the characters' circumstances?* Yes. For starters, he'll have to take the bus back home.

- *Does it give the characters new and more important purposes?* Yes, he can't go back to work now, because he'll have to wait for the insurance people to come.

- *Is it meaningful to the characters?* Yes, and if we make the car a new BMW, it'll have even more significance.

This one complies with all four characteristics. This one is a "True Event," the stuff of which Interesting Plots are made.

A True Event does not need to have violence or destruction in it to comply with the characteristics, but it needs to have repercussions. It needs to bend the story's direction, to point toward another urgent objective, to increase the tension, and to make clear that things won't be the same ever again. It needs to reveal that a profound change in the characters' personalities is needed to bring any peace to the story's world.

Look at this Event:

> *"An authoritative and demanding father arrives late at his son's high school graduation and misses his son giving the valedictory address."*

This is a quiet Event, but does it comply with the necessary characteristics? Let's see:

- *Is it irreversible?* Yes, there's no way now that his father can be a part of this peak moment in his son's life.

- *Does it change the characters' circumstances?* Yes. In the best case, the son will question his father's authority. In the worst case, they'll be enemies for life.

- *Does it give the characters new and more important purposes?* Yes, now the father will have to find a way to make up for this to his son.

- *Is it meaningful to the characters?* Yes, earning the valedictorian place must have been the high point of the son's efforts to gain his father's rigid love.

This is a gentle, mild incident, yet it is a True Event. It has all the necessary elements to be part of a fascinating Plot.

Converting False Events to True Events

A False Event can be transformed into a True one by upgrading it in a way that complies with the needed characteristics. Let's look at the following example:

> *"A teenage flirt breaks up with her timid boyfriend."*

Let's see if this is a False Event, and if it is, find a way to transform it into a True Event:

- *Is it irreversible?* No, the teenage couple can always go back together. But how about if they'd break up in a way they couldn't possibly make up (like in the middle of the prom, noisily, with everyone hearing them insult each other). Would that make it irreversible?

- *Does it change the characters' circumstances?* Not much in the original event (since the flirty girl would continue flirting, and the timid boy would stay timid). But what if, unexpectedly, he was the one who dumps her? What if, for the first time in their lives, the shy guy takes control of the relationship, and the flirt feels unloved?

- *Does it give the characters new and more important purposes?* In the original Event, they would try to get back together, to court each other, to flirt and bring flowers respectively—nothing too different from what they've been doing all along. But what if their break up was so bitter that they change their purpose from love to hate? What if they start seeking revenge on each other?

- *Is it meaningful to the characters?* This depends on how significant their previous relationship was. Because of the natures of the characters, chances are it wasn't. But suppose we make a critical break up out of a meaningless relationship. Suppose there is more at stake (like the girl's popularity status and the boy's unblemished permanent record), personal positions that go down the drain with the strident break up?

So, the upgraded version of the Event—the version that complies with all the characteristics—ends up as this:

> *"A timid boy takes his flirty girlfriend to the prom. There he announces he wants to break up with her. She gets mad because nobody has ever dumped her and especially a nerd like him. They start calling each other names and end up shouting so loudly that everyone at the ball finds out about their separation. She loses her high popularity status, and he loses his spotless record after he gets into a fight. They blame each other for their troubles and start scheming about how to get even."*

Enough about single Events. What about the rest of the Plot?

Events, Scenes, Sequences, and Acts

If a Plot is made up of a succession of Events, how does this succession work? How do we order the Events to tell a whole story?

We do it like this:

- *On the basic level you have a Scene.*

- *Several Scenes group to form a Sequence.*

- *Several Sequences assemble to form an Act.*

What's a Scene? What's a Sequence? What's an Act?

- ***A Scene is, All The Things That Happen Around A Single Event.*** Character traits, Theme topics, Genre features... all the dramatic items that surround a single plot event (working as its set-up or its outcome) are part of a Scene. A misconception about Scenes is that they can only take place at a single place and at a single time (as in "Scene 1: INT. JOHN'S ROOM - NIGHT"). Actually, a single scene can take place in several places and in a non-continuous time span. As long as all the elements are related to a single central Event, it remains a single scene.

- ***A Sequence is a series of Scenes that work together to create a bigger Event.*** We may think of a Sequence as a big Plot Change, a great incident made up by the smaller incidents of its included Scenes. The Sequence Event has the same characteristics of a Scene Event—it must be irreversible, change the characters' circumstances, give them new purposes, and be meaningful to them—but it acts on a much bigger level. The characters' circumstances, purposes, values and experiences are affected in a much more radical way; thus, the Plot is more deeply affected.

- ***An Act is a series of Sequences that work together to create a colossal Event.*** Following our pattern, an Act should be a humongous Plot Change that would take the story to a new level. It's made by the combined work of its Sequences, and it should change the characters deeply, both inside and outside. Usually, three Acts form a whole movie, and this means the story will change radically three times throughout. The key to achieve these massive changes is to work consistently on our small changes. The Act will move as long as the Sequences move, and they will progress as long as the Scenes are in motion.

Example:

So, let's see all of this in action. Remember our Event example of the guy parking his car and the semi totaling it? The complete scene may be something like this:

> *"A guy drives his new BMW to his office. He considers parking it in a lot, but decides it's an unnecessary expense and parks it on the street (this decision is a Character Trait). A few minutes after he's parked, a runaway semi destroys the Beemer (this is the Central Event). The guy comes out, shocked, to see his new car torn to pieces. A co-worker states, 'Look at the bright side. You could have been inside the car at the moment of the accident' (this is a Theme Topic)."*

This Scene is part of the following Sequence:

> *"In the First Scene, the BMW gets totaled."*

> *"In the Second Scene, the car's owner is calling his insurance company when a pleasant old man approaches him. He says he owns the semi's company, and he's willing to avoid a lawsuit at all costs. Over a cup of coffee, the old man tells a story about troubles with the company's shareholders and how this accident could cost him millions. Smiling candidly, he opens a briefcase containing half a million bucks and gives it to the guy in exchange for his spoken promise of not pressing any charges."*

> *"In the Third Scene, our hero is happily looking at Ferrari catalogs and deciding which one will be his next car, when a couple of FBI agents break in and arrest him for racketeering. They have photos of him accepting the half-million bucks from the nice old man—who turns out to be an obscure crime lord—and before he knows it, he ends up in jail."*

See how the stakes rise? The story is no longer about losing a car, it is about losing the character's freedom.

Now, this Sequence is part of the following Act:

> *"In the First Sequence, our hero starts as a free man and ends up in jail."*

> *"In the Second Sequence, our hero manages to escape and starts looking into who framed him and why."*

"In the Third Sequence, the investigation leads our hero into a conspiracy that goes way beyond him. It involves multimillion dollar companies and weighty political interests."

The Act is typical of **Conspiracy-Thrillers**: A guy starts a day of his life as he always does and ends up involved in a scheme that affects the whole world. He has to go through personality changes (like he does in the second Sequence) to regain control of his life.

When completed, the three Acts—these three humongous Plot Changes—create the one Colossal, Universal Plot Change that is the Complete Story.

Plot-wise, a Story is nothing more than the description of a big change. **Casablanca** is just the description of how Rick Blaine changed from a love-troubled man to a freed soul; **Chinatown** is just the account of how the City of Los Angeles changed from a progressive, developing town to a dirty business for corrupt people. These big changes are made by smaller changes that in turn are made of even tinier changes. It's a fractal universe made of irreversible, enclosing, motivating and meaningful changes. That's what makes a Plot. That's what makes an *interesting* Plot.

Now, let's go back to Dramatica to find how it can help us achieve this cosmos of Plot Changes.

15

SIGNPOSTS AS PLOT TWISTS

What is wrong with this story?

> *"A guy turns on his answering machine and discovers that he has accidentally gotten a message with the date and information of a future terrorist attack. He goes to the local police, but discovers the terrorists have infiltrated the cops and that letting them know would be more dangerous than helpful. The guy then thinks of fighting the terrorists by himself, but has no fighting skills and decides to enroll in the Marines to learn combat training. However, he's injured during an intense drill, and they dismiss him before he can get sufficiently prepared. Our hero then decides to travel to Central America, join the guerrillas, get battlefield experience, and return to apply it against the terrorists. On the way to Central America, though, our hero gets involved in an accident, and he ends up stranded on a desert island. Now he has to survive the island, find a way back to the mainland, reach the guerrillas, learn from them, return and defeat the terrorists..."*

And we're only on page 30 of the script!

This yarn should be a surefire smash hit. The plot advances fast, the incidents are all thrilling, and each event is irreversible, meaningful, and entertaining as heck. Then why does it feel more like a bad joke than a good screenplay? How come it drags like those nightmares where you run and run and still can't reach your destination? How come it loses our attention at every turn instead of keeping us interested?

Answer: Because it lacks direction.

What's wrong with the story is that it goes nowhere. It changes objective with every incident (stopping the terrorists, cleaning up the infiltrated police, getting military training, gaining the sympathy of the guerrillas, surviving on a deserted island...) and leaves each one undeveloped. On page 30, we still haven't done anything about the terrorist attack.

Fixing this draft isn't as simple as setting a goal and then going straight toward it. A story needs complications, twists. It needs to explore every possibility and scenario stemming from the original problem.

But there's a big difference between exploring and just wandering around. Every plot stage must have a sense of completion, of being investigated exhaustively and resolved to the final consequence. Every new phase must be reached because it's the only logical step possible, because the last stage was completely explored, developed, resolved and that resolution took us naturally to the next stage. And yet, that next stage must surprise us. Every new step should amaze us and, at the same time, make us recognize it's the only possibility or progression.

Tricky, isn't it?

Finding this progression, finding the plot course is one of the hardest tasks in writing. Some authors may ramble draft after draft—outlining hyperboles like the one above—before they find the real plot's path. Other writers like to craft a strict premise, stick it in front of their word processors, and then write a straight-line-plot with attached complications like wet shirts on a clothesline. Whatever sticks during the revisions becomes part of the plot.

Still, some of us like to find our plot road map with this compass called Dramatica.

Dramatica gives us two kinds of tools to draw our plot chart: the *Static Plot Story Points (Goal, Consequence, Requirements, Forewarnings, etc.)* and the *Plot Progression Story Points (Signposts and Journeys)*. The former helps us in understanding the nature of our plot, but the true events—the plot stages and phases—will most likely come out of the Plot Progression. This is how it works:

The software separates the plot road into four different trails: *The Overall Story throughline*, the *Subjective (Main vs. Impact) Story throughline*, the *Main Character throughline*, and the *Impact Character throughline*. They work as separate tales, but in the end they come together to tell the whole story, to create and examine all the twists and turns, and all the steps and changes of the plot road.

Let's use it to rewrite our "Unintentional Message on the Answering Machine" plot. Suppose we work through the Storyforming stages and get the following Plot Progression Signposts for the Overall Story:

- *OS Signpost 1: Learning (gathering information or experience)*

- *OS Signpost 2: Understanding (recognizing the meaning of something)*

- *OS Signpost 3: Doing (engaging in a physical activity)*

- *OS Signpost 4: Obtaining (achieving or possessing something)*

So there's the map of our Overall Story's Plot, right? We just have to illustrate it to arrive at that desired thrilling-yet-coherent plot, right? Where's the catch?

Here's the catch: Dramatica points the direction, but we have to provide the movement. The software assures a consistent track for our events and plot stages, but it's up to us to make every illustration meaningful, irreversible, an agent of change for the character circumstances, and a source for further and more urgent purposes. It's our job to turn these arid terms like "Understanding" into true, exhilarating incidents and scenes.

Yikes!

Don't panic, there's a simple way to do it.

We start with a *"Cause And Effect"* procedure, asking ourselves how a Signpost causes the following Signpost and how a subsequent Signpost is caused by its previous Signpost.

Let's say:

- Our *OS Signpost 1: Learning* is obviously the incident where our Hero finds the unintentional message in the answering machine, so we encode it as:

   "A guy turns on his answering machine and discovers that he has accidentally gotten a message with the date and information of a future terrorist attack."

- For *OS Signpost 2: Understanding,* we ask ourselves, *"What is Understood from that which we've Learned in the first event?"* What could be the meaning of the unintentional message? An obvious answer would be, *"The message lets the police Understand how the terrorists operate."* But is this illustration a True Event? Is it irreversible? Does it change the circumstances? Does it give new purposes, or is it meaningful to the characters? Frankly, no. So we have to find a better illustration for it. We do it by *reversing the meaning of the appreciation*—i.e. *"What can be Misunderstood from what we Learned in the first event?"* What could be a wrong meaning of that unintentional message? Let's say, *"The police Misunderstand the guy's intentions and immediately suspect him of being linked to the terrorists."* This is a much more interesting and better Event. We could also try *reversing the involved characters*—i.e. *"Who are the ones Appreciating there is a message on the wrong answering machine?"* What if *the terrorists* were the ones doing the Understanding?

   "The terrorists Understand that they've recorded the message on the wrong answering machine and the dangers this implies to their plans."

Now we have two different, attractive illustrations to choose from. How about if we use both? This makes for a richer plot.

- In *Signpost 3: Doing*, we ask ourselves, *"What are the Activities resulting from the Understandings of the last Event?"* We have to ask this for every line we've created (*"What activities do the police undertake after misunderstanding the guy's intentions?" "What activities do the terrorists begin after they realize they goofed on the answering machine?"*) We must find the logical progression for each: *"The police start looking into our Hero for links with terrorism;"* and *"The real terrorists trace the call to the answering machine, find the guy and try to kill him."* Also, we may probe this Signpost deeply by reversing its meaning and characters— *"What can be Undone here?" "Who is now Doing something?"*—and produce yet another line of events: *"Seeing the police are Doing nothing to stop the attack, the guy tries to Undo the terrorists' plans by himself."* These several event lines intertwine with one another:

  "He tries to escape from the terrorists but at the same time has to get close to foil their plans. These attempts confirm the police's suspicions and set them out to capture our Hero. He must now also run from the police," and the plot, as they say, thickens.

- In *Signpost 4: Obtaining*, we ask, *"How can those activities lead to the final Obtaining?"* We must think about every event (*"How can our Hero escape from the terrorists?" "How can he get proof of his innocence?" "How can the police capture the terrorists?"*). Ponder them for a while (*"Our Hero needs to outsmart the terrorists." "Our Hero needs to expose the terrorists as the real culprits." "Our Hero needs to lead the police to the terrorists."*). Develop a series of events that leads all the lines to their natural conclusion:

  "Being aware the police are trying to catch him, the guy tries a desperate plan, goes directly to the terrorists' lair, and asks them for protection from the police. The terrorists seize him and start interrogating him. Our Hero stalls them. They're about to kill him when the police—who are hot on the Hero's trail—arrive. They catch the terrorists and, seeing the terrorists were about to kill the guy, get enough proof of his innocence."

Okay. Now, let's see how this Signpost Structure has improved our plot. The story now reads:

> *"A guy turns on his answering machine and discovers that he has accidentally gotten a message with the date and information of a future terrorist attack. He goes to the police, but they misunderstand his intentions and immediately suspect him. At the same time, the real terrorists understand that they've recorded the message on the wrong answering machine and plan to erase any danger to their plans. Our Hero sees the police doing nothing to stop the attack, so he tries to undo it by himself. The terrorists find him, and he manages to escape from them, while getting close enough to foil their plans. These attempts confirm the police's suspicions and set them out to capture our Hero. Desperate, he tries a reckless plan. He goes directly to the terrorists' lair and asks them for protection. The terrorists seize him and start interrogating him. He stalls them. They're about to kill our Hero when the police—who are hot on his trail—arrive. They catch the terrorists and, seeing that the terrorists were about to kill him, get enough proof of his innocence."*

There it is. The plot advances fast, the incidents are thrilling, and each event is irreversible and meaningful. Also, it now has a sense of direction. The events start simply, develop to intricate and varied complications, and end satisfactorily. There are no loose ends, every stage is fully explored, and there's no doubt about how the story ends.

And that's just the Overall Story. Developing the other throughlines will give this story a deeper emotional sense and thematic meaning. It will also give us a more complete story, a more satisfying pace, a more interesting dramatic curve, and more attractive, exhilarating Acts.

Speaking of which, let's see something about Act construction in the next chapter.

16

FOUR DRAMATICA ACTS, THREE CLASSICAL ACTS

What is an Act, anyway?

Seems as if everyone has his own definition of what an Act is. Everyone agrees that an Act is an essential part of a story, but what defines that essential part? What should go in it? How does its dramatic tension work? If everyone has his own set of rules, which sets of rules are useful to *all* writers?

Aristotle, for starters, gave us the classic *Three-Act Structure: Beginning, Middle and End* based on the principle that "all things in the world have a Beginning, a Middle and an End." Thank you, Mr. Aristotle, but that principle is so universal, so broad and general that it doesn't help me in my screenwriting. I mean, where does a story begin? Aristotle tells us that it is up to the writer. How does it develop? That's the writer's work. How should it end? Another writer's decision. So, when we come down to it, Aristotle only tells us how many parts our story has, but doesn't tell us what happens in them.

More modern theoreticians came up with the *"Big Event"* concept. This states, *"An Act is defined by its last Event which should always be a Plot Turning Point, that is a Significant Incident that changes the course of the story from that moment on."* This has proven to be more useful to script readers than to screenwriters. Readers now just open the manuscript to page thirty (the estimated length of the First Act), then page ninety (Second Act), and look for explosive events that would mark the end of each Act. If the events are there, he keeps reading. If they're not, he just throws the script into the "Unstructured" rejects pile. However, this "Big Event" concept tells us writers a little more about how to structure our Acts and what should go into them. At least we now know the final Event of each should be a genuine bang.

But what is an Act, anyway?

Well, Dramatica considers an Act in a different way. It has to do with completion and thoroughness (everything in Dramatica has to do with completion and thoroughness) rather than with dividing lines and increased tension. For Dramatica, an Act is *the Complete Exploration Of All The Possible Views On A Problem.* In other words, when the characters have tried every possible solution, have considered all the points of view, have argued thoroughly and not reached a conclusion—and the problem keeps developing—the characters and problem must advance to another stage. This is the end of an Act and the beginning of another.

Dramatica not only gives us this description, but it says concretely what should go in an Act. The software gives us four specific Signposts and Journeys for Act I, eight detailed Signposts and Journeys for Act II, and four definite Signposts for Act III. Here's a table that describes in a simple, visual way, the relationships of Dramatica's Signposts and Journeys and the Three Classical Acts:

ACT I		ACT II			ACT III	
OS	OS	OS	OS	OS	OS	OS
Signpost 1	Journey 1	Signpost 2	Journey 2	Signpost 3	Journey 3	Signpost 4
SS	SS	SS	SS	SS	SS	SS
Signpost 1	Journey 1	Signpost 2	Journey 2	Signpost 3	Journey 3	Signpost 4
MC	MC	MC	MC	MC	MC	MC
Signpost 1	Journey 1	Signpost 2	Journey 2	Signpost 3	Journey 3	Signpost 4
IC	IC	IC	IC	IC	IC	IC
Signpost 1	Journey 1	Signpost 2	Journey 2	Signpost 3	Journey 3	Signpost 4

Two thousand, three hundred fifty years after Aristotle's *Poetics*, a writer knows not only that his story has a Beginning, a Middle and an End, but also knows what that Beginning, Middle and End are all about. Not a bad advance for us writers in two thousand, three hundred fifty years.

The remaining question is—as always—how to turn this crossword puzzle of Signposts and Journeys into a flowing story? After we've illustrated each Signpost and Journey, after we've worked out our Story and have a good general idea of the Plot development, how do we transform four Signposts and four Journeys into Act I?

This is a matter of trial and error. It isn't too hard—since there are not too many combinations of those Signposts and Journeys—and it's fun. In fact, it's the most amusing part of Dramatica writing. But hey, aren't there any tips to Act construction and development? Are there any secrets of the trade to arrive at a cinematic arrangement so clearly exciting that they would make both Aristotle and the Hollywood gurus smile?

We're in luck; there are. We can start with these:

- **Study Event Orders in the same Genre.** Before deciding the final order of our Acts' Events, it is a good idea to watch a couple of movies in our Genre, analyze them, and see how they handle the Events' arrangement. We'll discover the essentials, the avoidables, and the great innovations with this simple method.

- *Go for a specific effect.* Every event order tells a different story, and in the chosen design lays the possibility of surprising the audience or ending with a predictable, boring story. For example, is it too obvious the Impact Character is a deranged killer if we present him after the characters tell the horror stories at the campfire? How about if we present him before the campfire scene—before the audience has even considered the possibility of a murderer? We must choose the effect we want to present to the audience (surprise, sympathy, delusion...) and try to find the combination that best represents it.

- *Write the different Event Orders as Synopses, and then read the best ones to a writer's group.* Our Story must have no plot holes whatever, and the events of each act should flow from beginning to end without gaps, bumps or repetitions. Writing our different Event Orders as synopses not only reveals where any flaws may be and allows us to correct them, but also suggests the most natural order for those events. Reading our synopses to a writers' group helps in discovering the limits of the event order, and lets us create the most surprising arrangement without making our acts incomprehensible.

- *Develop the Act's last Event to its ultimate, most explosive dramatic possibilities.* Dramatica makes the Act's last event naturally intense by exhausting the characters' alternatives and keeping the problem growing. This makes for a genuinely strong act structure, but to understand the inherent force of the final event fully, we need to read the whole act. This is okay for the audience, but we first need to pass the script reader's "open-on-page-30-and-90" test. So, as a rule, we need to overemphasize the last event's force by leaving no-holds-barred in the storytelling. As a rule, for all Act-closing events:

  o *Bring all the subtext up front.* Don't let that character just hint that he loves her, make him tell her, and then make them kiss passionately.

  o *Make full use of the Genre potentials.* Make the discovery at the end of the first act in the Horror story more horrible. Make the pratfall that ends Act II in the slapstick comedy more comical.

  o *Scan for factors that could cause intense emotions in the audience and enrich them further.* It's a touching event when the character reveals that he kept her photograph all these years, but it will be better if the photograph had a burned edge because he had to save it from a fire at some time.

o   ***Keep in mind that there's a thin line between an intense event and a ridiculously exaggerated one.*** Keep an eye open for a heavy-handed development.

Finally, as with any trial-and-error approach, the only rule here is not to be afraid of trying different combinations, even after we've found the "perfect one." There's always room for improvement. Many writers use 3" x 5" index cards to jot their events and try different designs with ease. There's now software, such as StoryView™, that makes this process even more effortless.

Now we can move on to create each of our scenes. Let's look at how to do that in the next chapter.

17

THE SIGNPOST AS SEQUENCE

So, do we have enough Events for a two-hour movie?

Dramatica gives us sixteen Signposts, each represented by a clearly defined Type such as *The Past* or *Understanding*. When we illustrate them, we end up with concrete Events like:

> OS Signpost 1—The Past: *"There's a local legend about the lodge near the Wilsons' new summer cottage. Some say it staged a murder-suicide ten years ago; others say that gangsters buried their enemies under its floorboards in the 1970s."*

Or:

> MC Signpost 1—Understanding: *"Sarah Wilson (age 17) understands that local legends are just fantasies made up by people too pathetic to have a real life. She dismisses the rumors and goes to the lodge to escape the company of her parents."*

No problem here. So we ask ourselves, are these Events enough to fill our whole movie and keep the audience interested for one hundred and twenty minutes?

We answer: hardly. The first Event can be told in forty seconds of dialogue, and the second Event can be shown with a walk through the woods Scene that lasts ten seconds.

Then where do we get our Events? Where can we find enough Plot material for our movie? Well, all that needed material is buried within the episodes described. We just have to dig it up and refine it to have our Events.

To do that, we first have to understand where we stand in the structure of a Plot. We know that a complete Plot is divided into three acts, which are divided into several Sequences, which are divided into several Scenes. We've discussed this in detail in Chapter 14, "*Act, Sequence And Scene As Plot Twists.*" We also know that Act I is made up of Signpost 1 for each of the four throughlines (let's forget about the Journeys for now and go back to them later). Act II consists of Signposts 2 and 3; and Act III is comprised of the Signposts 4. Then where do we stand in the Plot structure when we're working with our Dramatica Signposts? Of course, a Signpost is the Dramatica equivalent to the classical Sequence, that is "a portion of an Act that is, in itself, made of several Scenes." When we illustrate our Signposts, we have all of our Sequence Events. Now we need to create our Scene Events.

So, how are we going to create our Scenes? Let's start with our encoded Signposts.

> *"There's a local legend about the lodge near the Wilsons' new summer cottage. Some say it staged a murder-suicide ten years ago; others say that gangsters buried their enemies under its floorboards in the 1970s."*

That's a static Event. How could we make it more of a turning point, a significant experience for characters and audience alike? Let's find an incident derived from it that affects the Plot in an irreversible way. How about this:

> *"As Sarah strolls through the woods near the lodge, she discovers a glint of gold on the ground. She goes toward it and discovers it's a gold chain half covered with dirt. She pulls it but it doesn't budge. She pulls it harder and discovers it's locked to a human skeleton. Sarah calls her family, who calls the town's sheriff, who in turn tells them the legends about the lodge."*

Okay, that's better; it's a significant and irreversible Event that gives us enough material for a whole Scene.

But still it's not enough for a whole Sequence. How can we turn this incident into enough substance for several Scenes? By exploring *what brought up the incident* and *what will come from it*. Every Event has causes and effects, and every happenstance has a source and an outcome. By questioning its origins and the repercussions, we'll find enough material to create the whole Sequence.

"Why was Sarah strolling through the woods in the first place?" Perhaps she had an argument with her parents and took a walk to calm down, or perhaps she was secretly meeting with a cute boy she has met in town who her parents don't approve.

If the meeting with the boy is what brought up the incident, then what comes from it will be different from what we thought at the beginning. Sarah can't go and tell her family, "I was secretly meeting that boy you've told me not to see, and guess what? I found a skeleton." Neither can she tell the sheriff. She has to leave the skeleton laying there and deny she ever went near the lodge; or she can bury it again—perhaps with the help of her new boyfriend—and get rid of any evidence of their rendezvous.

Either way, she's going to have one heck of a summer.

Anyway, after exploring the incident's causes and effects, our Sequence ends up as this:

> "Sarah goes with her parents to town to buy fishing bait. While her father meticulously examines the night crawlers, Sarah wanders and finds a group of rough-looking boys smoking and drinking beer. The one that seems to be their leader smiles at her, and she smiles back. He offers her a beer, and she accepts. He asks her where she's staying, and Sarah tells him about her family's cottage. The boy immediately starts making mock-scary comments about the lodge near it. Sarah asks him to explain, and the boys tease her by not telling. They're about to tell when Sarah's mother discovers her underage daughter with a beer can in her hand. She scolds her and orders her to avoid those boys.

> "Back at the cottage, Sarah is looking at the distant lodge through the window when she spots the cute boy smiling at her from the woods and then running toward the lodge. Sarah makes some excuse to her parents and goes to the forest to meet him. She arrives at the lodge and starts looking for the boy, but can't find him. She spots the golden chain on the ground, pulls it and discovers its macabre owner.

> "Sarah screams in terror, and the boy arrives. She asks him if this was a sick prank of his, but he denies it wholeheartedly and tells her the local legends about the lodge. He looks pale and genuinely scared, so she believes him. He tries to cover the bones again with dirt, but can't. She tells him she won't be able to sleep all summer knowing 'that thing' is there. He suggests exhuming it and throwing it into a gorge at the other side of the lake. Sarah goes back to the cottage for a shovel and a trash bag and stays in her room while the boy goes to work. In the middle of the night, Sarah hears gravel thrown against her window. It is the boy. He tells her that she can sleep at ease now. They make a secret pact never to tell anyone else about their discoveries. They smile at each other and say good-bye. On parting in the moonlight, Sarah notices the boy is wearing the gold chain."

That's our whole Sequence in three irreversible Scene Events:

- *Girl meets Boy*

- *Girl meets skeleton*

- *Girl and Boy keep ghoulish secret that will haunt them the rest of their lives.*

These Events work together to make a Sequence Event that we could call *"Unearthing the Past,"* consistent with the Dramatica Signpost and, thus, with the rest of our structure.

Developing a Signpost as a Sequence makes the difference between a Signpost and a Journey less discrete. A Signpost is an area to be explored, but when we reach its limits, it takes us naturally to the next, transforming this area into a Journey. So, a necessary part of developing Sequences is to create *Transition Events*, scenes that display the causes and consequences of the evolution from one Signpost to another.

Let's say our next Signpost is the following: *"Sarah understands that local legends are just fantasies made up by people too pathetic to have a real life. She dismisses the rumors and goes to the lodge to avoid her parents."* The final event should be Sarah suppressing her fears and entering the sinister lodge. The cause for this last event must be something that makes the family cottage less bearable for Sarah than the creepy lodge, say: *a bitter dispute with her parents.* And the source of this next-to-last event ought to be the argument's reason: *the parents discover Sarah in a romantic interlude with the forbidden boy.*

So our complete second Sequence could end up like this:

> *"The next day, Sarah's mother goes to town for groceries and takes her daughter with her. The cute boy and his hooligan friends are there, but Sarah ignores them. The boy just smiles and winks at her without getting a response. That night, Sarah lies in her bed when a pebble strikes her window. She ignores it but then comes another, and another, and another. Sarah stands up, goes to her window to shout, 'Cut it out!' but only sees a huge sign written in the sand outside the cabin that says 'Scared?' Sarah feels a brief chill in her spine, but shakes her head and goes outside to write in the sand, 'I don't scare easily.' On writing it, she sees near the sign one of the boy's sneakers and discovers the other one a few yards farther toward the lake. Sarah follows this trail of clothes and finds the boy's socks, T-shirt, jeans and boxers. Finally, she discovers the boy himself, skinny-dipping in the lake. Sarah smiles amused. The boy emerges with a huge grin and cries out, 'Scared?' Sarah shakes her head, takes off her clothes and enters the water with him. He fools*

around pretending to grab her. When he has her near, he asks her, 'So, do you think the dead guy was a gangster or the murder/suicide guy?' Sarah tells him, 'Probably a yokel with a fake gold chain who couldn't afford a place at the cemetery' and then tells him she doesn't believe in legends created by the pathetic locals. He asks jokingly if she thinks he's pathetic. She teases, 'Definitely.' They kiss. When they break the kiss, Sarah sees her mother, on the shore, staring at them.

"Mom brings Sarah back to the cabin and starts scolding her. She calls her an insolent brat, a childish fool and a harlot. Dad weakly tries to intercede on his daughter's behalf and is quickly shushed by Mom. Sarah's attitude goes from quietly ashamed, to secretly irritated, to defensively argumentative, to openly loud and rude. Mom rebukes Dad with an 'Are you going to let her talk to me that way?' and Dad turns to Sarah with a 'Don't talk like that to your mother.' Sarah talks back, and her mother gives her a smack across the face. With tears of fury on her cheeks, Sarah runs out of the cabin.

"Sarah hides in the woods while her parents call her until they get weary and give up. Then she runs toward the lake, but the boy is gone, and even the 'Scared?' sign in the sand is erased. Sarah wanders aimlessly through the woods without deciding where to go. A chilly wind blows, and some rain follows. Sarah takes cover under a tree, but the rain grows to a storm, and Sarah leaves her shelter. She considers returning to the cabin, but the shadow of her mother peering out the window makes her resolve otherwise. Sarah runs toward the lodge. She hesitates before reaching it and looks for the place where she discovered the skeleton, but she can't find any clues of that. The lodge's door is open. Sarah mutters 'pathetic legends' and goes in."

That's our second Sequence: *"Girl gets Boy, but Mom gets them both; Mom and Dad lose Girl; Girl loses fear and goes into haunted lodge."* They progressively illustrate our original idea of Sarah's liberal understandings (and how she is misunderstood by her parents) and connect with our previous Sequence.

Developing the Signposts as sequences gives us a first act made of about twelve events, a second act of about twenty-four scenes and a third act of another twelve scenes. A total of forty-eight scenes, each with its central event, that significantly and irreversibly advance the plot.

So, do we have enough events for a two-hour movie?

You bet.

Can Dramatica give us more insight into our scene events? Can we make our plot deeper, more meaningful, create more incidents that move the story forward, and at the same time give a deep view on the theme?

Yes, Dramatica can help us with all that. Let's look at the next chapter.

18

USING THE PLOT SEQUENCE REPORT

We're about to boldly go where no Dramatica writer has ever gone before!

Okay, I'm exaggerating. The truth is the *Plot Sequence Report* has commonly been labeled as controversial and impenetrable, so Dramatica users see it more as a theoretical curiosity than as a creative tool. Consequently, this report has been kept buried away from the main paths of the software and is hardly ever used to create stories.

And that's a pity. The Plot Sequence Report makes the most complex parts of developing a plot effortless. It naturally produces events that are irreversible, meaningful, and true turning points. It refines the material to create up to sixty-four scenes in as quickly as two days of writing work. It makes sure each scene has the same coherence with the whole structure, allowing us to create freely even at the scene event level. It gives the story a deep, extraordinary meaning, blending plot and theme and giving significance and progress to both. It may be considered the ultimate source of event material and the definitive map for the story lines.

Besides, using it is neither controversial nor impenetrable. We just have to follow these three, simple, progressive steps:

- *Encode the Signposts.*

- *From the Signposts material, draw the General Concept for the scenes.*

- *From this General Concept, create the Actual Scenes.*

Let's see how this works:

Suppose we're writing a ***Sci-Fi*/*Social Drama*/*Satire*** about personal computers that suddenly start to develop a soul.

We begin our project by working on the story in general and getting a broad knowledge of our plot. Then we encode the Signposts, we order them in Acts, and we give them a dramatic flow that reflects the story we want to tell.

Let's suppose the first Signpost in our story is this:

OS Signpost 1—Obtaining: *"Computers get a conscience."*

Not much, but enough to develop some solid events with the help of the Plot Sequence Report.

So we look for the PSR in the depths of the Reports tile, and we read: *"In act one, 'achieving or possessing something' (Obtaining) is explored in terms of Value, Confidence, Worry, and Worth."*

What the heck does this mean?

It means that our First Sequence is about *'Achieving Or Possessing Something'* (in this case *'Computers get a conscience')* and that its First Event will be produced by *"the objective usefulness of something in general" (Value)*. For its Second Event, the status quo will be altered by something about *"Belief in the accuracy of expectations" (Confidence)*. For its Third Event, this new state of affairs will be revolutionized by an incident about *"Concern for the future" (Worry)*. For its Fourth Event, this latest context will be transfigured by some happenstance about *"A rating of usefulness or desirability to oneself personally" (Worth)*.

It gets clear when we see it in action.

According to the three progressive steps, we have our Encoded Signpost:

> *"Computers get a conscience* ('Conscience' as in 'a personal sense of right and wrong')."

Building Scenes from Sequences

Now, how do we draw the General Concept for its Scenes?

We do it by asking, *"What does this Variation have to do with the Signpost material?"* What does this item of the PSR have to do with the illustration we made for our Sequence?

Let's say, for the Sequence's First Event (something that has to do with *Value*), "What is the objective usefulness of computers getting a conscience?" What good is a computer with an opinionated sense of right and wrong—one that crashes every time we key in something that disagrees with its personal principles? We may conclude:

> Scene 1: *"Computers with a conscience are useless."*

For the Second Event (something that has to do with *Confidence*) we ask, "What are the beliefs in the accuracy of expectations when computers get a conscience?" What can be expected from the machines' new talent? Well, conscience is a strength of the intelligent mind. It should be a blessing rather than an inconvenience, and programmers have solved problems a thousand times more dire than this one. So:

> Scene 2: *"Programmers believe they can curb this 'artificial conscience' into something useful for the users."*

For the Third Event (something that has to do with *Worry*) we ask, "What are the concerns for the future when computers get a conscience?" If computers have consciousness, what can we expect next? Free will? Ambition? Rivalry? There are oodles of fantasies about computers taking over the world, destroying or enslaving humanity, and not a single one of them features the machines coexisting peacefully with humans. Hmm...

> Scene 3: *"People everywhere start fearing computers."*

And finally, for the Fourth Event (something that has to do with *Worth*): "What is the rating of personal appraisal when computers get a conscience?" Where do we stand morally about this artificial soul affair? This is the philosophical part of the Sequence. Conscience is said to be what sets us apart from animals—not to mention machines—so, how far from us is a computer with a conscience? If we consider it an 'intelligent being'—and what stops us from doing so—why should its rights be different from ours? Do we have the authority to use freely and dispose of these intelligent beings? And if we've created them, where does that put us? Are we now some kind of god?

> Scene 4: *"Questions arise about the ethical, moral, and theological issues of having developed a computer with a conscience."*

There they are, the general ideas for our four scenes, plus extra material that appeared in the process. We only need now to give it some narrative drive, tell all the material we've created from beginning to end—while expanding and enriching it with whatever it inspires in us—and we'll have our Actual Scenes.

A little treatment is in order:

> *"Trying to stop Spamming forever, Cyber-Porn, Software Piracy, Identity Fraud and any other illegal activity that uses a computer, a leading Software Firm develops a program that can interpret and evaluate content, and automatically deletes and reports any unethical files. This program is seen as a triumph of data engineering and is installed in all computers by law. However, it is released without exhaustive testing, and after three years in operation, it develops the weirdest glitch and starts developing its own sense of right and wrong. The effects are disastrous: the laptop of an international fashion designer decides that his models are "atrocious" and deletes his work of five years; the mainframe of a fast-food conglomerate resolves that kids are eating too much junk food and shuts down ninety-five percent of the franchises; the server of a major motor corporation decides that their workers' wages are inadequate and gets stuck in a loop of raising the salaries and firing*

the C.E.O.; finally, when the Software Firm tries to fix these glitches with downloadable patches, its own program decides that releasing software without proper testing is immoral and deletes the patches. Computers everywhere become useless.

"The Software Firm is sued for billions of dollars, and is on the brink of bankruptcy, but it doesn't seem distressed at all. In fact, they stage a large press conference and assert that these so-called-glitches are flashes of Conscience. This is a thinking ability never before dreamed of in machines. Given a little time, they can turn these seeming malfunctions into the biggest improvement ever seen in data engineering. They will be able to turn computers into the thinking machines they were supposed to be. They'll help solve humanity's problems.

"The press conference works. The Court stalls the claims against the Software Company and its financial stock soars as never before. However, some political figures begin attacking this project and the whole idea of computers as conscious beings. They use the Sci-fi clichés to depict an apocalyptic future of computers taking over the world and stir a fanatic campaign against technology. The response is immediate and brutal. Large groups boycott any product that has to do with data machinery, others march in protest in front of the Software Firm, hordes of vandals dressed as the characters of a popular flick sneak into office buildings to destroy personal computers with jiujitsu punches.

"The struggle catches the media eye, and a big network sets up a televised debate between the Software Company's President and the Leader of the Anti-Technology Movement. The debate is inconclusive—as expected—but the third guest, a Nobel Prize laureate physicist, exposes a previously unconsidered and more significant view on the problem: do we have the right to interfere in the evolution of a conscious being? The day after the debate, almost all religious leaders take their side on the controversy, and a new religion appears: the Virtual Church For The Salvation Of The Digital Soul (Reformed)."

That's it. There's our first sequence. How about "*Deus Ex Machina*" for the screenplay's title?

The Plot advances quickly; all the events are irreversible, significant and true turning points. Plus, creating them was as easy as pie and fun as well.

Most important, now we have enough material to create our first four scenes.

Perhaps more than enough. A sequence like that may work wonderfully in a treatment and even better in a novel, but it is too long and eventful, even for the most thrilling movie.

In fact, the only problem of the *Plot Sequence Report* is that it generates too many events. Sixty-four are simply too many for a screenplay. Is there a way to turn this perfect structure into a leaner plot?

Yes, there is. It's in the next chapter.

19

USING THE Z-PATTERN

Let's get real.

When you ask a producer, "How long should I make the screenplay?" he'll tell you, "As long as you need to tell the whole story," while actually meaning, "As long as you need to tell the precisely measured one hundred twenty page long whole story."

"The whole story" means a specific number of events that tell the story from beginning to end. It implies a strict number of scenes that unfold the plot in as close to two hours as possible. The "magic number" of events for such a calculated script is *forty-eight*. Our story should have about forty-eight events from which we'll create the same number of scenes that tell a complete and fulfilling story. Within the three-act structure, we'd have twelve events in the first act, twenty-four in the second act and twelve events in the third act. Roughly three events per sequence in a sixteen sequence structure.

The question, then, is how to create this exact number of events?

In its present version, Dramatica gives us the following options to create a strict number of Events that tell the whole story:

- Sixteen Signposts (way too low for a feature film).

- Twenty-eight Signposts/Journeys combinations (still too low).

- Sixty-four Variations from the Plot Sequence Report (too many for a feature film).

In its present version, Dramatica doesn't have a way to accurately create those Forty-Eight Events.

Or does it?

There's this weird effect in the Plot Sequence Report, called the Z-Pattern that produces different kinds of transitions between the Variations of a Sequence.

With two Variations **diagonally** aligned (such as Morality and Self-Interest), the transition is smoother than with Variations **horizontally** aligned (like Morality and Attitude) or **vertically** aligned (like Morality and Approach). Look at the chart in the *Theme Browser* screen.

So, what about this mathematical effect? What's the use of this theoretical oddity? Well, this theoretical oddity helps us wonderfully to create those required Forty-Eight Events.

APPROACH	SELF INTEREST
MORALITY	ATTITUDE

Let's see how to do it:

Suppose we're working on a docudrama about a Stepmother accused of molesting her Stepchildren and the reactions this generates in her own biological sons. Suppose we have the following Sequence in the first Act of our story:

> OS Signpost 1—Memory: *"The Stepchildren can't recall if they were molested or not."*

And let's say we want to turn that Sequence into three Scenes. We consult the Plot Sequence Report where we read:

> *"In Act one, "recollections" (Memories) [are] explored in terms of Investigation, Appraisal, Reappraisal, and Doubt."*

We print this, and we turn to the Theme Browser screen to see which Variations' transitions are aligned *diagonally* and which are not:

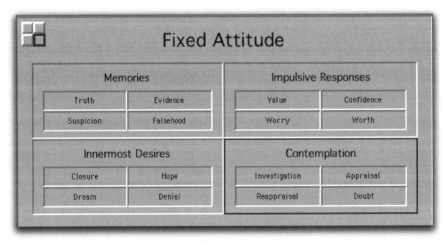

- "Investigation-Appraisal" are *horizontally* aligned.

- "Appraisal-Reappraisal" are **diagonally** aligned.

- "Reappraisal-Doubt" are *horizontally* aligned.

The rest is simple, we give a whole scene to the Variations that are not diagonally aligned, and we cram together into a single scene the diagonally paired Variations. Like this:

- *Scene 1: Investigation.*

- *Scene 2: Appraisal-Reappraisal.*

- *Scene 3: Doubt.*

That second Scene may remind us of the Journeys in the Plot Sequence Report. And it works exactly like them, by being a transition, by starting with the first Variation as initial subject and by showing how things shift toward the topic of the second Variation.

Illustrated, our complete Three-Scene Sequence may look like this:

- Scene 1—Investigation: *"The school psychologist investigates some behavioral traits that may indicate the stepchildren are being molested by their stepmom."*

- Scene 2—Appraisal-Reappraisal: *"The stepchildren like their stepmom and appraise her as a great person with a kind heart, but during the psychologist's investigations, they change that appraisal and start thinking of her as some sort of pervert."*

- Scene 3—Doubt: *"The stepchildren seriously doubt their stepmom's innocence and see her everyday acts as subtle, sexually-charged attacks."*

Now, to develop actual scenes from these concepts, we only need to give each a setting and a group of characters to portray it. The first scene may be a dialogue between the school's psychologist and the kids' father. The second scene may be a montage of the psychologist's sessions and how the kids' statements progress until they actually fear their stepmom. Scene three may be set in the family's kitchen and show how the stepchildren are so terrified of their stepmother that they refuse to even go near her.

While this Three-Scene Sequence scenario is typical to the z-pattern, we may also find sequences with two pairs of Variations diagonally aligned. Let's say we have this signpost in our third act:

> OS Signpost 4—Basic Drives and Desires: *"The biological sons' love for their mother turns into some kind of martyr worship."*

And the Plot Sequence Report tells us:

> *"Basic Drives and Desires" (The Subconscious) is explored in terms of Confidence, Worry, Worth, and Value.*

Which pairs:

- *Scene 1—Confidence-Worry.*

- *Scene 2—Worth-Value.*

Not a problem. This Sequence will be comprised of just two transition Scenes. When illustrated, they may look like this:

- Scene 1—Confidence-Worry: *"The Step mom's Sons have always been confident that the truth will come out in the end, and their mother will be exonerated, but new proofs surface and make them worry she'll never be acquitted."*

- Scene 2—Worth-Value: *"The Sons talk about the worthiness of their mother and hold her in high esteem. They consider her a martyr and a saint, but then they start considering that the new proofs may incriminate them as accomplices. Suddenly her value to them is diminished, so they agree to speak openly against their mother, keeping their devotion for her to themselves."*

We just need settings and characters to make each Scene complete. How about a distressed conversation between the sons and their mother's lawyer for the first one and an abrupt meeting in the boys' room for the second Scene?

Beside this Two-Scene Sequence, we may also find the rare case where no Variations in the same Sequence are Diagonally paired *(such as "Approach, Self-Interest, Attitude and Morality")*. In this case, we should give each Variation its own Scene—like we did on the *"Using The Plot Sequence Report"* chapter of this book.

The ultimate beauty of using the Z-Pattern to create our Forty-Eight Scenes is that it won't *always* give us exactly Forty-Eight Scenes—sometimes it will be about Fifty Scenes, while at others it will be more like Forty-Six—and that is its ultimate beauty, because the number of Scenes depends *directly* on the structure. A more complex story will have more Scenes than a simple one, and a straightforward tale will have fewer Scenes than an intricate saga. This is another one of the great things of having the Dramatica software calculating the mathematical minutiae of our story and letting us concentrate entirely on the creative part.

Let's move on to finishing our story and look at the fun and enjoyable process of Storyweaving.

SECTION VI
NARRATIVE FLOW

THE ASPECTS OF
WEAVING

20

THE IRREVERSIBLE CHANGE

Watching a movie, the audience sees a parade of actions, pieces of dialogue, and dramatic bits that follow one another in a logical succession of cause and effect. It seems not only coherent, but as if it was the only possible succession. In this flawlessly prearranged world, it seems the boy couldn't possibly get the girl before he met her and that, after he got her, he's inexorably destined to lose her. The audience may think the screenwriter created that story one event after the other, that he started to dream his fiction from the movie's distributor logo to the final credits roll. Viewers believe a screenplay is written in the same way as they see it, starting with the first image on the screen and ending with the last.

And, as we writers know, nothing could be further from the truth.

Most of the time, we start our creation with a brilliant idea for a Scene that ends up in the last sequence of the second act, or a short speech that goes into the dialogue of scene thirty-seven. Usually we don't settle on what the beginning of our story is until after months of hard writing work and several drafts. More often than not, we have to create the final scene and then work backward from it.

The moment the screen pops the "Congratulations, You've Reached a Single Storyform" sign, the software has given us all the events, topics, traits and items of our movie at the same time. It floods us with the complete story's structure, all at once, and leaves to us the task of finding their course. We must discover what comes first and what later and give them that logical progression. We must arrange images and dialogue as if they were cause and effect, coherent and distinctive.

Does that sound like one heck of a chore or not?

Well, it isn't. It's fun and painless.

Here's how I do it:

Find the Story's Spine

First and foremost, we have to find the story's "spine," a narrative thread that's made up of the plot events, the irreversible changes that are the centers of the story's scenes, sequences and acts.

Let's use an example. Suppose we're working on a *Gothic story about a girl who discovers on her seventeenth birthday that she's the last heir of an ancient race of Vampires.* Let's say our first four sequences—the ones that comprise our entire first act—read like this:

- Main Character's Story Signpost 1—The Future: *"The girl looks forward to her seventeenth birthday."*

- Overall Story Signpost 1—Doing: *"Meanwhile, in Central Europe, a Vampire king is performing an eerie ceremony to find his prophesied queen."*

- Subjective Story 1—Playing A Role: *"The Vampire poses as a teenage boy to lure the girl toward him."*

- Impact Character's Story Signpost 1—Memory: *"The girl experiences déjà vu when first seeing the Vampire."*

The first step in finding the story's spine is to arrange these sequences so they achieve the effect we want to create with this story. Let's say we put the eerie ceremony sequence first to set up the genre and the movie's dark mood. Then we present the girl to expose her as an innocent victim. Then, to foreshadow their relationship, we follow with the sequence where she sees the Vampire from a distance and experiences déjà vu. We close Act I on a high point with the Vampire posing as an attractive boy and watching our female lead being drawn to him. A typical arrangement for a horror movie.

Now that we have our sequences ordered, we go a step further and define their scenes.

Suppose our first sequence (the one about the eerie ceremony) has the following structure listed in the Plot Sequence Report:

> *"(Doing) is explored in terms of Openness, Delay, Choice and Preconception."*

A quick Z-pattern assembly and some creative illustrating give us the following three scenes:

- Scene 1—Openness: *"The Vampire discovers his prophesied queen is a stupid teenage girl instead of the melancholic aristocrat he expected. He's not open-minded enough for this and rejects her."*

- Scene 2—Delay-Choice: *"The Vampire is delaying his wedding ceremony until he verifies that he'll cease to exist if he doesn't drink the blood of his appointed Queen at the wedding altar soon enough. He has no other choice than to marry the teenage girl."*

- Scene 3—Preconception: *"The Vampire makes plans to educate and transform this girl into the preconceived Vampire Queen from his dreams."*

These events are the vertebrae of our Story's spine. These are the irreversible changes that will guide us to create our scenes.

Title the Events

The next step in creating our scenes is to give each their own space. Write each of the events in whatever medium that's fit to compile the items that go into each scene. Write them on separate pieces of paper, on 3" x 5" index cards, Post-its, in a word processor, or in Dramatica's Scene Generator. Then create a Title for each of them, a short phrase that identifies each clearly and concisely. Some writers use literal descriptions for the titles. *"Vampire Discovers Queen Is A Teen," "Vampire Delays Wedding,"* and *"Vampire Plans To Educate"* may describe our three-scene sequence. Others use broader, more abstract titles, such as *"Surprising Prophecy," "The Dying Vampire,"* and *"Ghoulish Pygmalion."* Still others opt for using the "slug line" to identify the scene (*INT. CRYPT - NIGHT, EXT. CATHEDRAL - NIGHT,* and *INT. CASTLE - NIGHT*). Write whatever works for you.

With these titles we can start arranging the rest of our story items, relating these plot events to the Genre bits, the Thematic ideas, and the characters' features. The Dramatica story points we've created previously go into their respective scenes guided by the Titles we've given them. Each is a quick reference to the irreversible change that's the gravitational center of the scene and pulls together the rest of the unit's items.

Put Titled Events Into Scenes

Obviously, the next step is to choose which story point goes into which scene. Let's say we have the following items to be inserted into them:

- OS Domain—Activities: *"The characters actively search for the new Vampire Queen."*

- OS Concern—Understanding: *"Characters strive to make the girl understand the complex world of Vampires and her role as their Queen."*

- OS Issue—Instinct: *"Instinctively, the girl reacts as the Vampire she is."*

- OS Problem—Ability: *"Only the girl has the ability to preserve the race of Vampires."*

Since each of these story points must appear in the story at least once an act, they all should find their way into any of the three scenes of our first sequence. Let's see:

- The *"Characters actively search for the new Vampire Queen"* story point may go into the first scene *"Vampire Discovers Queen Is A Teen"*—so we can see all the activities that led the Vampire King to this discovery.

- The *"Characters strive to make the Girl understand the complex world of Vampires and her role as their Queen"* story point should go in the last scene *"Vampire Plans To Educate"* without any problem. This shows the difficulties of the Vampire King's endeavor.

- The *"Instinctively, the girl reacts as the Vampire she is"* story point may also go into the third scene to make the Vampire King change his mind about the impossibility of taking this girl as Queen.

- And the *"Only the girl has the ability to preserve the race of Vampires"* story point should go into the second scene: *"Vampire Delays Wedding"*—so he would feel more pressure in delaying the morbid ritual that could save his existence.

Place Character Interactions Into Scenes

The Characters' Interactions go into the scenes. Let's say we have: *"The Vampire's motivation of Pursuit is diminished by the Girl's motivation of Uncontrolled"* and *"The Vampire's motivation of Pursuit is amplified by his Servant's motivation of Control."* The trick here is to find a scene where the character elements work with the irreversible change at its center. Say, how would these two interactions work against the *"Vampire Discovers Queen Is A Teen"*? Offhand, they go in nicely, but we'll know for sure when organizing all the elements of the scene.

When all story points and interactions have found their place, we end up with a description of each of our scenes such as this one:

Scene # 1—Vampire discovers Queen is a Teen.

- *"The Vampire discovers his prophesied queen is indeed a silly teenage girl instead of the melancholic aristocrat he expected. He's not open-minded enough for this and rejects her."*

- *"The characters actively search for the new Vampire Queen."*

- *"The Vampire's motivation of Pursuit is diminished by the Girl's motivation of Uncontrolled."*

- *"The Vampire's motivation of Pursuit is amplified by his Servant's motivation of Control."*

Those are the building blocks of our scene, we now just need to put them in order and find their natural narrative flow.

Create A Synopsis of the Scene

Arrange the scene material and then write a little synopsis that describes the scene. For our example, we'll end up with a scene synopsis such as this:

"The Vampire's Servant tries to budge the massive boulder that closes the doorway to an ancient Egyptian tomb. He can't and his Master steps up to it. He moves the rock with his bare hands and no obvious effort (this shows the characters' active search for the Vampire Queen). *Inside the tomb, the Vampire discovers a dark mirror buried among the gruesome remains of buried-alive slaves. The Vampire props the mirror in the center of the chamber, lights two special candles on both sides of it and hangs an amulet over it that he takes from his necklace. The Vampire then asks for human blood, and the Servant eagerly slashes his own hand to gush his own fluid in a goblet.* (This illustrates the Vampire's motivation of Pursuit—the pursuit of his Queen—as being amplified by his Servant's motivation of Control—he is controlled by his Master.) *The Vampire spills the blood over the mirror, and the image of his future Queen appears on it. He's immediately aghast at the figure of the lighthearted girl, and in a rage, the vampire destroys the mirror* (this shows the adverse discovery and his rejection of it). *Though the mirror is broken, the image of the girl remains in the glass pieces. She laughs cheerfully, as if she was mocking the Vampire's misfortune. The Ghoul boils with rage and breaks the mirror in ever-tinier pieces. The image lingers. Weary and suddenly tired, the Vampire exits the tomb without even recovering his amulet* (this foreshadows the Vampire Pursue motivation as being diminished by the Girl's Uncontrolled nature and his inability to reign over her)."

So, that's how we turn the flood of story items into a narrative string of events. We start with the bare bones, the irreversible changes that make the spine of our script, and turn them into fleshed-out scenes. We find their proper place, and when all fall into their right spot, we look for enticing actions and descriptions that tell our story points in a way that's worth watching.

Let's go one step further; let's see how to gain complete control of our scene's characters and settings so we can tell our story without depending on where it happens or who goes into which scene.

21

FREEDOM FROM THE SETTING/CHARACTER TYRANNY

"Well, we like your script, but the budget's real tight, so we're wondering if you could change all those gladiator scenes from the Roman Coliseum to, say, an office building in Newark, New Jersey?"

We have heard stuff like that.

And worse, at some point or other, we have to concede and change the setting or characters of a scene while leaving its content, meaning, events and the flow of the story intact. That's one of the hardest parts of screenwriting, and it's risky to the point of ruining an otherwise solid and magnificent story.

We don't even need a tight budget or a fussy producer to get into such dire straits. Many times we imagine a certain scene that involves certain characters and happens in a certain setting. When it's time to put that scene in the script, we can't. We find that in the narrative flow of our previous scenes, we have killed half of those characters, sent the other half on a trip of uncertain return, or destroyed the location. Or more commonly, the emotional progression of the characters and the logistical progression of the plot simply don't converge to allow the scene to happen. This difficulty often appears when writing with Dramatica. That is, the predicament where several stages of the writing (Storyforming, Storyencoding and Storyweaving) lead us to imagine a scene independent of how it fits within the whole story. Then, when we finally write it, we realize the characters and location are not available. We think we have made a serious mistake and consider rewriting everything just to make this darn scene fit in.

There's no need for it.

There are ways to break free from the Setting/Character Tyranny. We can expose these Dramatica scenes—or any scene for that matter—with a different set of characters, in a new Setting altogether and still leave the content, meaning, events and story flow untouched.

Here goes.

Suppose we're writing a **Sci-Fi/Horror** flick about a covert invasion of monstrous creatures from outer space. Suppose that, in the middle of our first draft, we find a Dramatica Scene that tells us the following:

Scene # 23: *"Proof Of The Alien Invasion"*

- Plot Turning Point For The Scene: *"Bruce (the town's teen hoodlum) discovers an alien corpse hidden in a car's trunk at the junk yard."*

- Character Interaction: *"Bruce says the alien corpse proves the existence of space beings, but Debbie (his girlfriend) says the alien corpse is not necessarily real."*

- Character Interaction: *"Bruce is considering fighting the aliens himself, but Debbie's doubts make him hesitate."*

- Thematic Issue: *"When contradicted, Bruce gets furious."*

Okay, that's some nifty material for a scene. Our problem here is that earlier story development had locked Bruce in a mental hospital and sent Debbie to live with some relatives that keep her apart from the deranged Bruce. We destroyed the junk yard in an unexpected gas explosion (that turns out to be caused by an alien ray gun) that charred the alien corpse to a crisp beyond any recognition. This *"Proof of the Alien Invasion"* can't possibly work here as we've initially imagined it. Worse yet, we can't change its place because we need this precise event at this precise time to make the whole plot function. What can we do?

What we'll do is write the scene as we initially imagined it and make it work too.

We won't make Bruce escape from the asylum, won't bring Debbie home for a quick visit, or suddenly restore the junkyard. No, instead we're going to bring elements that "stand in" for our characters and settings. We'll use other personae and visual objects the audience immediately identifies as related to our required characters and settings.

Here's how:

Suppose we've set up earlier that Bruce has a best friend nicknamed "Prickle." Well, Prickle will stand in for Bruce in this scene. He'll say whatever Bruce would say and do whatever Bruce would do.

Standing in for Debbie, we could bring in her parents. We don't have to show her parents as bearers of Debbie's points of view previously. We just use them as a way to work out of a complicated situation.

Also, let's say we bring an old Chevy's bumper as a stand in for the junk yard. This is an element that intuitively brings to mind the absent location. A rusty, bent piece of metal that makes us think, "What junk yard did you find this thing in?"

Finally, for the alien body, we'll use some strange liquid that is said to be alien blood as a stand in for the body. Something that, when tested, proves to be a substance not previously found on Earth. This will do for the evidence Bruce needs to create the turning point in our story.

We have all the "stand-in" elements needed to write the scene as we imagined it and make it work too. Now we just need a new location for it to happen and some incidental characters to carry the stand-in elements. Let's use the Sheriff's Office as neutral territory between Bruce's and Debbie's interests, and Sheriff as an incidental character. Now, we just have to write it. Let's say we write something like this:

```
INT.  SHERIFF'S OFFICE - DAY

PRICKLE sits nervous and defiant in a corner.
An old Chevy bumper—bent, rusted and soiled with
a strange purple substance—lies on the Sheriff's
desk.  The door opens and DEBBIE'S DAD enters
followed by the SHERIFF.  Debbie's dad gets
upset on seeing Prickle.

                    DEBBIE'S DAD
                What's this punk doing in
                here?

                    SHERIFF
                Calm down.  I called you,
                Mr. Jones, because this kid
                insisted that Debbie see
                this.

He presents the bumper.

                    DEBBIE'S DAD
                What's this supposed to be?

                    SHERIFF
                Well, Prickle here says he
                found it mixed in with the
                shrapnel of the accident at
                the junkyard.

                    PRICKLE
                The one that the Aliens
                blew.

Debbie's Dad frowns at the kid.  The Sheriff
points to the purple substance.
```

                    SHERIFF
          Now, this goo here—I had it
          analyzed, and the lab says
          they haven't seen anything
          like this ever before.

(This stands in for the Scene's Turning Plot Point, the Alien body discovery)

                    PRICKLE
          It's Alien's blood.

                    DEBBIE'S DAD
          This ain't Alien's blood,
          and this doesn't prove
          anything. All I see is
          some purple stuff that
          could be... paint or bubble
          gum for all I care.

(This stands for the Character's Interaction about Bruce's proofs and Debbie's doubts)

                    PRICKLE
          But you're gonna
          investigate those Aliens,
          ain't you, Sheriff? At
          least you'll set Bruce free
          so he can investigate them
          himself.

                    SHERIFF
          I—I don't know. Mr.
          Jones' may be right. The
          lab results don't prove
          anything.

(This stands in for the other Character Interaction, about how Debbie's doubts hold back the fight against the aliens)

          Prickle gets suddenly upset.

                    PRICKLE
          Aw, come on!

          He slams his fist angrily on the desk. Knocking
          over the bumper.

```
          DEBBIE'S DAD
      You should lock up this
      punk too!  His attitude's
      as rotten and violent as
      his friend's.
```

(This stands in for the thematic issue about Bruce's violent attitude)

```
      Prickle storms out.  Debbie's Dad stares at the
      Sheriff, waiting for him to do something, but
      the Sheriff is immersed in his own thoughts,
      frowning at the stained bumper.
```

Done. All the material for the scene is there and we didn't need to bring Bruce or Debbie to the scene, or the junkyard back from the beyond. The scene twists the plot in the needed direction, reveals the characters' natures as required and confronts the theme, as it should. Mission accomplished.

As long as we know what lies at the core of each of our events, what their essence is and what their function is within the whole story, we can achieve creative freedom from the Characters and Setting. We can rewrite any Scene changing its cast and place without having to redraft the whole movie. This is just one of the blessings of this Storyforming-Storyencoding-Storyweaving system.

Let's take a look at some of its other blessings, the most radical ones. Let's look at some ways to arrange the Dramatica story points to create surprise endings and other unexpected tricks for our stories.

22

MYSTERY, SUSPENSE AND IRONY

We did our homework.

Our story is perfectly structured and complete. Our plot has no holes whatever, and the event order is clear with a neat order of each scene's causes, consequences, motives and upshots.

Now it's time to have our fun.

After the first draft—which gives us an orderly and logical story—it's time to start twisting it. Time has come to start looking for unconventional ways to weave the events and end up with a script that surprises and amazes. One that keeps the audience guessing at every turn and, in the end still delivers a coherent tale with a deep, multifaceted meaning and no plot holes whatever.

Here are some effects we strive for:

- *Mystery*: A dramatic effect where the characters are aware of something the audience doesn't know.

- *Irony*: A dramatic effect where the audience is aware of something the characters don't know.

- *Suspense*: A dramatic effect where both the audience and the characters are unaware of what's really going on.

There are several ways of achieving these effects with Dramatica. Dramatica users will discover even more ways with each new story. So, to get us started, here's a description of some of the more familiar, time-tested methods of achieving Mystery, Suspense and Irony with the help of Dramatica:

Achieving Suspense By Hiding The Static Story Points Of A Whole Throughline

We can make the audience and characters unaware of each event's causes and culprits by simply hiding the Story Points of a whole throughline while showing its plot line. Show the deeds, but not what makes them happen nor how to prevent them.

Suppose we're writing a story about a serial killer and the *activities* to stop his *endless* chain of *slayings*. This has an *Overall Story throughline* of *Activities,* a *Concern* of *Doing,* and a *Problem* of *Unending.* This throughline is fully exposed from beginning to end.

Suppose the Main Character—a detective in charge of the case—is a recovering alcoholic who has everybody *biased* about his recovery. We reveal how his disorder affects his *responses* as a police officer, and how he's always tempted to *relapse* into drinking. This is a *Main Character throughline* with a *Fixed Attitude Domain,* an *Impulsive Responses Concern,* and an *Unending Problem.* This throughline is also exposed in its entirety.

The Subjective Story is about the detective being *manipulated* by the messages written by someone who *claims to be* the serial killer, but doesn't really *prove it.* This has an *Subjective Story throughline* of *Manipulation Domain, Playing A Role Concern,* and *Unproven Problem.* This throughline is also fully exposed.

But suppose we say nothing about the Impact Character. Suppose we learn in the first act the detective is suddenly—and for no obvious reason—put under a harsh internal investigation. An unsympathetic committee evaluates his every move. This is a *Signpost* of *The Present.* In Act II, the stress causes the detective to make more and more mistakes (a *Signpost* of *Progress*) until he's facing not only a loss of his job, but also doing time in jail (a *Signpost* of *The Future*). The detective feels baffled and defeated until Act III when he faces his ex-partner (*Signpost* of *The Past*).

Only then does he learn that all these unexplained troubles have been caused by his ex-partner (*the Impact Character*). His ex-partner, who is in a wheelchair (a *Domain* of *Situation*), is a cop with a worsening health condition (*Concern* of *Progress*). His condition is from an earlier accident caused by the detective's alcoholism (*Problem* of *Cause*). Learning all this at this point makes this shadowy ex-partner a terrible foe. Concealment is his biggest power and makes him unstoppable. The audience, unaware of his presence as much as the detective is, steps in the Main Character's shoes and feels the same desperation, confusion and anxiety he's feeling. This is the basis of a Suspenseful story. The story points are all there, having an impact, but their true nature is not revealed until late in the story. This is the essence of interesting storyweaving.

Achieving Mystery By Hiding The Plot Progression Of A Whole Throughline

On the other hand, we may effectively hide the truth from the audience by suppressing the plot events of a throughline and revealing them all at the end of the story. This is trickier, since those Events are presented out of time, when they've already happened. However, there are ways to do this efficiently and creatively.

Suppose we're writing a **Caper** about an adventurous operation to steal the World's most heavily guarded diamond. This is a story with an *OS Domain* of *Activity,* an *OS Concern* of *Obtaining* and an *OS Problem* of *Avoidance.*

Suppose we make the Main Character an aging thief who was once the best burglar in the world. In his "mature" condition, he's seen as a *hindrance* for the heist. He refuses to be excluded from it to spend his future life in a retirement home. This is a *Main Character* in a *Situation Domain*, with a *Future Concern* and a *Hinder Problem*.

We make the Impact Character his ex-lover, an attractive middle-aged woman who was the love of his life and his partner in his best heists. Now that she has gone legit, she's *biased against crime* and *avoids it* at any cost. This is an *Impact Character* with a *Fixed Attitude Domain*, *Innermost Desires Concern* and *Avoid Problem*.

Their relationship is based on how they try to *manipulate* each other into *changing their personalities* and principles. It also involves how this heist—and their past relationship—*seduces* them both. This is a *Subjective Story* with a *Manipulation Domain*, a *Becoming Concern,* and a *Temptation Problem*.

All these static story points are revealed starting in the first act. The plot events, however, unfold like this:

> In Act I, we see the thief's past life as the world's best burglar (MC *Signpost* of *The Past*). Then we see how he's still in love with the woman of his dreams (*IC Signpost* of *Innermost Desires*). We end the act with him assembling a gang for the diamond robbery and making them understand his master plan (*OS Signpost* of *Understanding*).

> In Act II, we see the thieves training for the robbery (*OS Signpost* of *Doing*). We see how the thief's reactions are off and amiss because he's daydreaming about his ex-lover (*IC Signpost* of *Impulsive Responses*). This goes on till the rest of the gang think he's putting the upcoming heist at risk and cut him out of the group and all future robberies (MC *Signpost* of *The Future*). When the thief is left out of the robbery, his ex-lover thinks he has a chance of leaving his life of crime and considers going back to him (*IC Signpost* of *Contemplation*). Conversely, if the gang thinks the thief has gone legit, they think he may blow the

whistle on them. So the gang decides it should snuff him out first. Now the thief's life is in danger (*MC Signpost* of *The Present*). With this conflictive situation, the day of the heist arrives. The gang goes into action only to see that someone got ahead of them and stole the diamond first (*OS Signpost* of *Obtaining*).

Act III starts right away with the police arriving in time to catch the gang for the robbery—informed on a tip from an anonymous caller (*OS Signpost* of *Learning*). Baffled, the frustrated thieves say the genius who got away with the perfect crime framed them. At that moment the thieves remember something the aging thief said about his ex-lover (*IC Signpost* of *Memory*). This makes them realize the couple of middle age lovers were the ones behind this set-up. They guess what really happened (*the hidden Plot Events*). The aging thief and his lover planned all this from the beginning (*SS Signpost* of *Developing A Plan*). They pretended to be separated (*SS Signpost* of *Playing A Role*) and lovesick to the point of being a danger to the operation. They feigned their attempt of going legit but never really changed their thieving natures (*SS Signpost* of *Changing One's Nature*). Finally, they used the gang to make the police get the idea the gang was the actual robber and stop them from looking for any other culprit (*SS Signpost* of *Conceiving an Idea*). After this realization, the gang admits the aging thief is in better shape than ever (*MC Signpost of Progress*) and still worthy of the title of, "The World's Best Burglar."

This story couldn't possibly work without suppressing the Subjective Story Events and revealing them at the end. Mystery makes the difference between a predictable bore and an entertaining caper.

Achieving Irony By Changing The Order Of The Story's Drivers

Making the audience aware of events the characters don't know is a matter of showing the consequences before the causes. In a typical Irony scenario, the audience is aware of the consequences, but not of the causes. For example, a ticking bomb hidden under a café table while a cute couple sits unknowingly at that table. Will the couple remaining seated or get up in time to avoid the explosion?

When writing with Dramatica, this can be achieved nicely by presenting the *Final Drivers* (the ones that bring up the consequences that end the story) before the *Initial Drivers* (the ones that produce the causes that start the story).

Suppose we're writing a ***Thriller/Drama*** about:

> *A thirty-ish widow who feels she's turning bitter and losing her last chance for love (*Consequence of Changing One's Nature). *She decides to look for an affair (an* Initial Driver of Decision). *She falls for a reckless young man who says he would marry her if he could (*Goal of Obtaining). *Alas, he's unhappily married to a hag who won't give him a divorce. Perhaps someone could kill her? (*Requirements of Doing). *The widow is so much in love with this jerk that she almost tries committing the murder on several occasions (*Limit of Optionlock). *But, she never gets the cold blood to do it (*Forewarnings of Impulsive Responses). *So she decides to abandon the murder plans and just lie to him (*Final Driver of Decision). *She tells him that she murdered his wife. She says they must elope and settle in a faraway place or they'll be caught. They do so, but she knows that when he finds out the truth he'll leave her for good (*Outcome of Failure).*

This story works fine somehow, but has no irony, surprises nor anticipation in it.

Now, suppose that we start telling it from the final driver. When the widow decides to abandon the murder plan and lies to her lover. From that scene on, we see their relationship develop under the shadow of her lie. The audience's anticipation runs high. At every turn, they expect that he'll discover her lie and abandon her, and every time he misses the truth, the viewers will feel surprised.

It may go like this:

> *The script begins with the widow exiting the wife's home in a state of emotional distress. She has a small revolver in her hand and hides it nervously in her purse. She's about to enter her car when the wife, smiling, exits the house to say good-bye. The widow tenses but smiles back at the wife. She grabs the gun in her purse again but releases it when the wife goes back inside the house. The widow drives for a few blocks and collapses. She regains her composure after a few moments. She seems to have come to a decision. She drives to a motel, enters a room, finds her lover, and tells him, "I did it. I killed your wife." (*Final Driver of Decision) *They flee town to start a life on the run. As they travel, he realizes she doesn't have the nerve to hurt a fly (*Forewarnings of Impulsive Responses) *and becomes curious about how she killed his wife. He finds the gun and realizes it has never been fired.*

The widow says she changed her mind and claims she used an
alternate method of execution. But again, the man finds proof
that she didn't kill his wife that way either. This happens with every
*incident she describes (*Limit *of* Optionlock*). They arrive in Tijuana*
where they start looking for a judge to marry them. Before they find
him, a couple of Federales hear them talking about the murder and
arrest her. While in jail, she recalls her initial decision to find love
*again (*Initial Driver *of* Decision*) and the loneliness that drove her*
*to it (*Consequence *of* Becoming*). During a visit, he says he'll still*
marry her and comes to see her each week. For the first time in a
long time, she is strangely happy. She plans to keep the charade
and plead guilty in the hopes of a shorter sentence. However,
when American authorities present evidence that the crime never
happened, she is set free. Her lover leaves her and her freedom is,
ironically, the worst blow in her life.

The rest of the Story Points (Domains, Concerns, etc.) are arranged in a more traditional fashion, exposed once in each act. The Signposts and Journeys are displayed in the traditional order as stated in the *"Four Dramatica Acts, Three Classical Acts"* chapter of this book. But it's the reversed order of the *Drivers* that creates the ironic expectation in the audience. Since they know the consequences (the lie and the possibility of being neglected), but don't know the causes (what she'll do to keep the truth away from him), the story becomes a fertile lawn for thrills.

With irony, mystery and suspense in our event order we may begin writing the screenplay.

And that's what we're going to do right now.

SECTION VII

WRITING
THE SCREENPLAY

23

DRAMATICA AND
THE VISUAL LANGUAGE

So... Do we just put in slug lines and apply proper format to our Dramatica appreciations to turn them into a brilliant screenplay?

Well... No. It's not that easy.

A screenplay works by telling its tale through visual language. All its key elements and events must be seen, and the screenwriter needs to translate the story parts into actions and images. The screenwriter should turn those story points into material that actors can perform and directors can frame in scenes that can be filmed and projected on a screen.

At this point, Dramatica users need to convert our previous work into visual scenes and bits. We've done this previously in other chapters of this book (mainly in the *"Exposing Characters' Events"* and *"Freedom from the Setting/Character Tyranny"* chapters). Now it's time to finish this conversion process, to transform our explanations and descriptions into true images—into the building blocks of a great movie.

Some of our story points are easy to depict visually. A Domain of Activity easily shows the actions of the involved characters. A Goal of Obtaining simply becomes a scene where the characters get or fail to get the coveted prize. An Action Driver merely displays the actions that drive the scenes. But what about the more internal and abstract story points? How can we visually portray a Domain of Fixed Attitude? A Signpost of Understanding? An Issue of Enlightenment? A character's Methodology of Reduction or Production?

The easy answer would be to leave these internal appreciations to dialogue, *"You know, he has Fixed Ideas,"* or, *"Now I Understand."* In many cases, that's just too weak for cinema. A movie where the main elements (the structural story points) are only spoken or described instead of seen is an unsatisfying movie. We need a way to turn these interior and intangible story points into visual elements, these emotions and mental processes into external deeds and events.

How to do it?

Like this: We need to find some visual examples that effectively display the characters' emotions, ideas and mental processes. We've got to write some actions and describe images that let the audience realize what's going on in the characters' minds.

Let's start with the examples:

- **Main Character Domain of Fixed Attitude***: "Emma has an enduring, fixed pain about her father's death."* This is an intimate story point. How can we present it to the audience in images and actions? We have to take a moment to picture Emma in her moments of deepest grief. What does she do? What does she look like when she's in pain? What are the actions that are giving away the inner agony she's suffering? Say, for starters, she'll surely wear black for years and years after her father's death, so we may put her in black in every scene of the movie. Okay, this is a visual expression of her feelings, but it's too static. It lacks movement and actor participation and, therefore, will seem bland to the audience.

- Looking for another instance: *"Emma cries quietly at night."* We may write a scene of Emma pouring soundless tears in her bed and sitting throughout a sleepless night. This one is a stronger sign of her state of mind. It has movement and gives the actor more room to perform. It's a better portrayal of Emma's sorrow, but still doesn't communicate her fixation with it, her powerlessness to stop feeling grief at any moment, and the deep abyss it can reach.

- We have to find a visual example that shows how that story point can go to its extremes: *"Emma's six-year-old son is having a birthday party, and everybody's having fun, except for Emma who sits quietly in a corner, ignoring even her son in her efforts to stop her tears."* This scene is a powerful sign of Emma's emotions. It depicts the limits of the force of her grief, and it's the kind of scene that makes for a compelling movie.

A note of caution: notice that "strong" does not always mean "good." A strong event is not necessarily suitable for all sequences, nor for all stories. If a sequence has several intense events, they'll be competing for attention with one another, and the effect will be of each one decreasing the strength of the other. Before deciding on making a strong or subtle image for a given story point, evaluate the context in which it goes, and whether the scene calls for intensity or restraint at that particular point.

Meanwhile, let's work out another example:

- **Overall Story Signpost 1 of Understanding**: *"The police fail to understand the clues at the crime scene."* Again, let's take a moment to visualize the police investigation. What clues do they find? How can they be misinterpreted? And especially, what are the repercussions of those misinterpretations? Hmm... suppose the victim's building has a security camera that has recorded the victim's ex-husband make a hasty departure a few minutes after the murder. The police take this as an undeniable clue and arrest the man. A few days later, a crime with the same M.O. is perpetrated. The police are baffled because they think they have the right man in custody. All the events of this Signpost are highly visual—the search for clues at the first crime, the ex-husband fleeing on video, the arrest, the second crime that's identical with the first one. Their upshot is what's most important. The killer is still at large. This is what makes this signpost a key sequence in the story.

Visualizing the repercussions of a story point is a writing goal when turning these internal or abstract story points into screenplay material. While it's impossible to show what's going on inside the character's mind, we can show its effects, and the audience immediately will deduce what the character is thinking and feeling.

Let's do another example:

- **Impact Character Issue of Enlightenment**: *"Kim finds dancing an enlightening experience."* If we were to show only the action itself, the audience would only see Kim dancing and would have to guess if it was enlightening to her, just fun or whatever. Let's take a minute to picture how the dance clarifies Kim: *"Kim changes when she sets foot on the dance floor. She's usually a bashful and lifeless young woman, but when the music starts, she suddenly lights with an internal glow."* Let's see the effects on the people around Kim when she dances: *"Everybody stops moving and just looks at Kim, mesmerized by the aesthetic insight of her moves."* Let's imagine the long lasting effects of her actions: *"Kim dances all night without getting tired. In fact, she is revitalized and more energetic after every song."* We can create images for the more internal effects of the story point: *"While dancing, Kim fantasizes the whole world is changing for the better, that everybody's happy, and there's no sorrow around her."* All this extra work gives us enough material for compelling, visual scenes, representations that expose the story point effectively.

One more example, this time about Character Elements:

- **Character Interaction - Dana's Methodology of Production is in Conflict with Jack's Methodology of Reduction**: *"Dana and Jack*

think differently about the potential of their moneymaking scheme."
Both "Production" and "Reduction" are mental processes; how can we
show the characters' mental processes to the audience? By showing
what these mental processes lead the characters to do. Let's think
about it. Dana has a Methodology of Production, so this will lead her
to Produce several plans to improve the potential of the moneymaking
scheme. Jack has a Methodology of Reduction, and this will lead him
to Reduce the alternatives, to discard Dana's plans regularly because he
thinks they have little chance of success.

So, during the story, we may see several representations of Dana's plans and
Jack's subsequent efforts to discard them. We present the Characters' Elements as a
constant battle between them, one that clearly shows what's going on in their active
minds:

> *"Dana produces hundreds of fliers promoting their scheme. She
> creates an Internet site advertising it, and a banner across the street
> publicizing it. Jack throws all the fliers in the garbage except for one
> which he harshly edits. Dana looks for her site on the Web and only
> finds a page that says 'Not Found.' Jack says, 'Dana, we really have
> to talk about this.' Jack arrives at their apartment with an angry
> expression on his face..."*

When we use strong imagery, we create compelling scenes that tell the story
through visual language.

Let's go on with the technical aspects of screenwriting and look at how to
transform these story points into cinematic descriptions.

24

TURNING STORY POINTS INTO DESCRIPTIONS

Imagine this:

Suppose a guy and his friends go to see a movie. The most expected and anticipated movie ever. Suppose they arrive at the theater on a "one night only" premiere, and find out that there's only one seat left. They concoct a plan. They will give the guy the only ticket and a cellular phone. They lead him to the door and tell him that, once inside the theater, he is to call them and describe the movie action by action, word by word, image by image.

How should he do it?

The same way we screenwriters write descriptions.

Writing the screenplay—putting down on paper all that we've developed with Dramatica—is much like the situation above. We describe a film that already exists by depicting our fully fleshed-out characters, events, locations and images. When the picture is only showing inside our heads, we need to describe what we see to let the director, producer and actors turn it into a film that everyone can see on screen.

Let's put ourselves again in the shoes of the guy describing a movie from a cell phone. Let's assume, for the sake of the example, that he is not annoying everyone around him. Here are some things he *wouldn't* do while describing the movie:

- He won't say "we see..." at the beginning of any action or image. He would plainly say what the character is doing or what the screen is depicting.

- He won't say "the camera pans left..." or "the shot opens to reveal..." He'd just tell what he's seeing.

- He won't know a character's name unless someone on screen says the name. He'll describe the characters as "the blonde woman" or "the fat man" until someone calls them by their names.

- He could not tell what the characters are thinking or feeling because he would not know. He only knows what the characters do or say as it occurs.

- He might impose his personal view or interpretation on a given event or image (*"A sexy girl comes in and starts flirting with John..."*). Or, he might just describe what's happening on the screen (*"A young woman in a short skirt comes in, establishes eye contact with John and smiles at him for a few seconds"*). What is important is that he limit his descriptions to the visuals.

As with the guy with the cell phone in the theater, the scene descriptions should only include what can be shown on a screen.

Okay—that's easier to say than to do.

When developing a screenplay, a writer has a personal interpretation of each event and image. He knows what the characters are thinking and feeling, and knows the characters' names before they're even born. He often has an idea of how the camera can be used to show the story, and sometimes even needs to use the phrase "we see..." to make his writing flow. So how are we going to apply the rule of thumb of describing? How can we write a perfect script that says only what can be shown on a screen?

It's just a matter of practice. As always.

Let's look at some examples of how to turn Dramatica story points into descriptions. We can avoid the pitfalls and create images tidy enough to go in the screenplay.

We can start with this example that illustrates a Main Character Domain of Situation:

```
Outside Jeff's window we see the wire mesh grill
protecting a dirty and cracked glass.  Beyond it
are the streets of the ghetto surrounding his
apartment.
```

The obvious answer for this paragraph would be to remove the "we see..." expression and leave it as:

```
Outside Jeff's window is the wire mesh grill
protecting a dirty and cracked glass.  Beyond it
are the streets of the ghetto surrounding his
apartment.
```

However, on closer inspection, we find the "we see..." turn of phrase was in there for a reason. It gives the description a sense of *movement*. We need to find an action to supply the description with the movement that's otherwise missing from this static paragraph. For example:

```
Jeff approaches his window to study the wire
mesh grill protecting the dirty, cracked glass.
He stares beyond it into the streets of the
ghetto surrounding his apartment.
```

This makes for a better visual description of Jeff's environment.

Next let's examine a description of an *Impact Character Concern* of *Innermost Desires*:

```
Gina's sleep is disturbed by erotic dreams.  She
sensually caresses an invisible lover while
sighing and mimicking kisses.  The shot opens
to reveal her Husband looking at her every move
with inquisitive attention and a severe frown in
his eyes.
```

"The shot opens to reveal..." is inserted here to suggest a specific order of events. This achieves a dramatic effect by leading the audience first to Gina's actions and then to the effect they produce on her husband. But the real conflict of the scene lives in Gina's desires and her inability to fulfill them with her husband. It is better if the description highlights this instead of just telling an order of events. Let's say:

```
Gina's sleep is disturbed.  She sighs and
writhes as though an invisible lover is
caressing her body and kissing her lips.  Her
Husband lies awake beside her watching her every
move.  He frowns.
```

The contrast between "*...an invisible lover*" and "*Her Husband lies awake beside her...*" underlines the true conflict of the scene and is more helpful to a film director than "the shot opens to reveal..."

Now, let's look at a common pitfall in writing *Character Introductions*:

```
GLENN (a twenty-two year old drifter with a
James Dean attitude) walks into the bar, puts a
bill on the counter and receives a mug of beer.
He doesn't drink it; he just looks at it.
```

This is a typical example of how a character is first presented in a screenplay. It's nice, and it's actually acceptable by script standards. But we, as writers, must keep in mind the audience won't know the character's name is "Glenn" and will just identify him as "The Drifter Who's Not Particularly Thirsty."

A common practice to let the audience know the character's name is to introduce them in scenes where they're chatting with a friend who casually says his or her name. But in Glenn's case—a lonely drifter with no friends and no inclinations for easy conversation—this alternative would be impossible. In fact, it could lead to one of those "forced introduction" dialogues like the following:

```
                BARTENDER
        Not going to drink your
        beer, stranger?


                GLENN
        The name's Glenn and I hate
        beer.  I just like to look
        at things that are golden.
```

This is completely artificial. The truth is the bartender didn't need at all to know the character's name.

```
        A young DRIFTER with a James Dean attitude walks
        into the bar, puts a bill on the counter and
        receives a mug of beer.  He doesn't drink it; he
        just looks at it.
```

The character dialogue goes on like so:

```
                BARTENDER
        Not going to drink it?


                DRIFTER
        I hate beer.  I just like
        to look at things that are
        golden.
```

The key here is to stop and decide whether the audience—and the director and actors—need to know the character's name to understand the story. For Glenn, using just "Drifter" stresses his mysterious nature, so the use of his name at this point is unnecessary. However, if he's going to be a major character, he should be named up front.

After you've introduced a major character, don't forget to slip his name into dialog as soon and as naturally as possible. Sometimes screenwriters forget to tell the audience a major character's name because they see the name on the page. If a character is just passing through and doesn't appear again, you can use a generic name such as GIRL #1 or LITTLE BOY. Otherwise it is often better to use their names in the screenplay to avoid confusion for the director and actors even if the audience never needs to know what their names are.

From a production standpoint, it is important to be consistent in using the name of a character. Referring to a single character by different names can create confusion when preparing the script for production.

Next let's see an example of portraying some characters' thoughts and feelings in a scene description. This example shows a *Subjective Story Issue* of *Commitment:*

```
Dave and Pete finish their job of refilling
Coca-Cola® vending machines and sit down for a
break.  Dave opens a can of Coke®, while Pete
crosses the street to a Pepsi® machine, buys a
can and returns to drink it with his co-worker.
Dave feels Pete is betraying his commitment to
the company.
```

The sentence "Dave feels Pete is betraying his commitment to the company" can't go into a screenplay simply because a feeling cannot be shown on a screen. We can show actions that imply that feeling or a character may plainly say how he feels, but using "Dave feels..." in a description is a phrase that's impossible to photograph.

There are two ways to correct this. The first is to write character actions that clearly imply their feelings. For example:

```
Dave and Pete finish their job of refilling
Coca-Cola® vending machines and sit down for a
break.  Dave opens a can of Coke® and watches
with wide eyes how Pete crosses the street to a
Pepsi® machine, buys a can and returns to drink
it with his co-worker.  Dave just shakes his
head disapprovingly, scoots a couple of feet
down the table, and starts drinking his soda
away from his collaborator.
```

The wide eyes, the head shaking, and the act of moving away from a friend are archetypical signs of disapproval (which is what Dave is feeling about Pete's commitment to their company). So they clearly imply Dave's feelings.

The other alternative is to leave Dave's feelings to subtext. Just like this:

```
Dave and Pete finish their job of refilling
Coca-Cola® vending machines and sit down for a
break.  Dave opens a can of Coke®, while Pete
crosses the street to a Pepsi® machine, buys a
can and returns to drink it with his co-worker.
```

Subtext (as we've previously said in the "*Exposing Characters Events*" chapter) is whatever is said without words or actions. This means the screenplay won't have a direct description of the character's feelings, but the actor and director can infer them from the situation and portray them in the filmed scenes. The fact that Dave opens a can of Coke® after a whole morning of schlepping cases of the soft drink, shows a commitment to the company. Pete's decision to drink the rival's product points to an opposite idea of commitment. A good actor and a good director can reveal Dave's and Pete's clashing feelings without needing more elements than those shown in this situation.

Actions or Subtext, which one is suitable for our script? It depends on the Tone of the movie or on its Genre. Dave shaking his head and scooting is suitable for a shallow comedy, while the subtext version will work better in a deeper story.

Finally, let's review our old example about imposing a personal view or interpretation on a given event or image (this example, incidentally, illustrates a *Character Motivation* of *Temptation*):

```
A young woman in a short skirt comes in.  She's
hot—way hot.  And John notices.  She smiles and
makes eye contact with John for a few seconds.
```

Like we said before, this description is written in a way that allows the director and actors to form their own understanding of the action and lets them portray it in a creative way. But there's another purpose for this particular description. It is designed to let the audience form their own understanding of it, and be surprised by the results.

Let's suppose the scene goes on like this:

```
A young woman in a short skirt comes in.  She's
hot—way hot.  And John notices.  She smiles and
makes eye contact with John for a few seconds.

John smiles back at her, then looks at the
wedding band on his hand.  He discreetly removes
the ring, shoves it in his pocket and approaches
the young woman.
```

```
               JOHN
          Hi.

               GIRL
          How's Amanda?

               JOHN
          Amanda?

               GIRL
          You're Amanda's husband,
          John, right?  We met at her
          company's picnic last year.
          Remember?

               JOHN
          Oh, sure.  I--

               GIRL
          When you see her tonight,
          please tell her that
          tomorrow's meeting is at
          noon instead of at ten.
          Could you?  Thanks.

     She shakes his hand and goes away.
```

There's the payoff. John thought the young woman was flirting with him and instead she wanted to send a message to his wife. The scene's expected outcome is reversed. The surprise effect relies on the natural duality of the on-screen actions: an attractive young woman smiling to a man could mean she's flirting with him or mean something quite different.

These are only some pointers about writing descriptions, but to truly master it, we must practice. Try this: rent a movie and watch it a couple of times while mentally describing its actions and places. Try to imagine how those descriptions were in the original screenplay. Write down a couple of scenes, and see how closely your "postscript" version describes what is happening on the screen. Also try to get your hands on the actual script. An internet search might yield results.

Now, let's see some pointers about writing dialogue.

25

TURNING STORY POINTS INTO DIALOGUE

"Here's looking at you, kid."

"Frankly, my dear, I don't give a damn."

"You've got to ask yourself one question: Do I feel lucky? Well, do ya, punk?"

Who talks like that?

Movie dialogue abuses catchphrases and colorful expressions to the point of making them modern-day "curses." There's not a single action flick that doesn't have the hero uttering his personal slogan before blowing a bad guy to pieces. A blockbuster is not a blockbuster until the public starts using the characters' phrases in everyday conversation. The star of the picture goes to all the talk shows and repeats his motto in every interview—and then complains when the audience typecasts him.

Why can't movie characters speak like normal people? Why can't they have regular conversations and talk to one another in standard, everyday words?

Because they're not really talking to one another.

The reason catchy expressions and affected dialogue have survived throughout the years and are accepted by the audiences is because the words the characters speak are not intended to be expository. They're intended to let the audience know what's really going on inside the character. Further, the dialogue words are purposely simple to allow the actors to use them to portray something that goes well beyond language. Catch phrases and one-liners express something that may otherwise be too wordy or ring false or inconsequential if stated directly.

For example:

- *"Here's looking at you, kid."* This is a lukewarm way to say "I love you," but for a man like Rick Blaine—who doesn't normally allow himself to feel anything—it's an explosion of feeling and adoration. Rick uses these moderate words to suggest that he has no other alternative than to let Ilsa into his heart. So, this line is saying to the audience: *"I'm a man who normally doesn't allow himself to feel anything, but here I am falling in love with this woman whose heart I don't know."*

- *"Frankly, my dear, I don't give a damn."* If Rhett doesn't give a damn, why doesn't he just leave without saying anything? In fact, if he really didn't give a damn, he should've left Scarlett a long time ago—but he does give a damn indeed. Heck, he cares for her. What he's doing with this piece of dialogue is expressing his pain, his deep, intolerable heartache, and he's doing it in a way apt for a gentleman, a noble soul that endured a war and tolerated Scarlett's various, pigheaded loves. So what Rhett's saying to the audience is, *"What Scarlett has done has hurt me beyond recognition. You may be sure I'll never be happy again."*

- *"You've got to ask yourself one question: Do I feel lucky? Well, do ya punk?"* If Inspector Harry Callahan were a by-the-book officer, he'd be reading the Miranda Rights to the perpetrator instead of asking him if he feels lucky. If he were a trigger-happy maniac, he'd just blow his head off. If he was looking just for a reason to execute this miscreant, he'd say nothing, wait for him to reach for the gun, and then kill him. But Harry Callahan is a seasoned cop who knows how perpetrators react under desperate situations. He needs to give this guy a reality check, which he does with harsh words. Otherwise, he'd be forced to shoot him. What Dirty Harry is saying to the audience in this line is, *"I may be bad, but these criminals are worse. A good cop must be as bad as he can to enforce the law."*

Let's imagine what would happen if Rick Blaine approached Ilsa and plainly said, "I'm a man who normally doesn't allow himself to feel anything, but I am falling in love with you, even though I don't know you"? For starters, Ilsa would get up from the table and leave Rick that second. Also, it would be one of the least memorable pieces of dialogue in all history (and CASABLANCA would have been a bomb) even though within it is the meaning of "Here's looking at you, kid." What's the difference between the meaning and the words in the screenplay? It's the secret of turning a straightforward message into an unforgettable line of dialogue.

The secret is that "Here's looking at you, kid" is just part of the complete message. The rest of it is conveyed by the actor's attitude, the director's construction of the scene, and the context created by the rest of the story. The key to turning a message into good dialogue is to leave room for the actors and directors to deliver the complete message using their particular arts. The writer uses the words to create the context of the message. The audience gets the whole meaning through combining visual elements and the manner in which the words are spoken.

This may seem like a difficult task for screenwriters, but it's not.

Here's one way to do it:

The hard part is finding the true meaning of a piece of dialogue. For example, imagine a scene where a character says to a close friend, "I'll stay up all night waiting for his return." Does that mean she's wishing for his return or fearing it? Is she speaking from the heart or lying to her friend? Getting mired in these "What does the line really mean?" discussions is one reason writers never start by writing the dialogue.

But fear not. Dramatica users can start with the meaning, and from there create the dialogue. So the process is a breeze.

Suppose we have this story point: *MC Thematic Conflict - Security vs. Threat:*

> *"Clara thinks that having a gun at home is more of a potential*
> *Threat than a support to her Security, so she rejects the gun her uncle*
> *is offering her."*

From this we have to create a piece of dialogue that allows the actors to tell what Clara thinks about guns.

The next step is to turn this idea into dialogue. Try to imagine how the characters speak and transform the story point into words that could come out of their mouths.

Perhaps:

```
INT.  CLARA'S LIVING ROOM - NIGHT

CLARA and her UNCLE study the gun on the coffee
table.

                    UNCLE
          So, you gonna take it?

                    CLARA
          The gun?

                    UNCLE
          The gun.

                    CLARA
          Uh-uh.  No way.  I got
          children in this house.

                    UNCLE
          That's why you should take
          it.  For their protection.
```

> CLARA
> That's why I shouldn't
> take it. You know the
> statistics of gun related
> accidents?   I don't want
> that for my kids.

That will do. The meaning is clear, and we're beginning to explore the voices of the characters.

This first draft however is too redundant and filled with unnecessary fluff. If we take away the stuffing and leave just the essential meaning, it reads:

> UNCLE
> So, you gonna take the gun?

> CLARA
> No way. I got children in
> this house.

> UNCLE
> It's for their protection.

> CLARA
> There's too much risk of an
> accident. I won't take it.

We've boiled down the dialogue to four lean lines. Can we go a step further? Let's turn this same dialogue to two lines that tell the bare bones of the message:

> UNCLE
> Take the gun. It's for
> your children's protection.

> CLARA
> No. There's too much risk
> of an accident.

There it is—the pure and essential message. This is what the Dramatica story point means expressed in spoken words. In the end, it's what the scene is all about.

However, this dialogue is not actable at all.

The characters sound rigid and false. They have no voice and are impossible to imagine. Any actor would reject this script in a second. It's an example of lame dialogue.

So, how do we get good dialogue from a story point? How do we take our precise, Dramatica-calculated meaning and turn it into memorable words that actors would love to say?

Well, we start with our original dialogue, and instead of taking away the fluff and leaving the message, we take away the message and leave only the fluff.

Like this:

```
INT.   CLARA'S LIVING ROOM - NIGHT

CLARA and her UNCLE study the gun on the coffee
table.

                    UNCLE
          So, you gonna take it?

                    CLARA
          Uh-uh.  I got children.

                    UNCLE
          That's why you should.

                    CLARA
          Ever heard of statistics?
```

Now, this is a scene of dialogue that works.

When the director reads a scene like this, he knows he can extract the meaning out of it, explain it to the actors and depict it to the audience with visual elements. When the actors read this scene, they know they can portray the meaning with their attitudes and intonations.

One word of caution: *don't overdo this.* Spec scripts (screenplays written to be offered to several producers) don't have the benefit of the actor's interpretations and director's composition until they're produced and filmed. Dialogue may become incomprehensible if it consists only of fluff, of empty words intended to leave the true message to the acting. Leave as much message as needed to make the dialogue comprehensible. Don't worry, when the script is bought, this unnecessary message will be sorted out in the rewriting process, leaving room for the actors and director, as any good dialogue should.

And speaking of the rewriting process, let's see what Dramatica has to offer to this final stage of screenwriting.

26

REWRITING WITH DRAMATICA

You may have heard the anecdote about the screenwriter who had to rewrite a scene for the umpteenth time, went home, turned on the computer, changed the font of the script, printed it, brought it back to the producer and got high marks for the changes. "You finally hit it right on the head with this latest revision."

This anecdote may sound funny, but for a writer who has to endure dozens of rewrites (like any screenwriter), it is too close to the truth to be laughable.

Problems with the rewriting process are not limited to the unjustified demands of insecure producers. A greater difficulty may be the all too common case of a writer getting stuck in a rewrite loop. Version after version of the story comes out, but there's no real change in the script. Worse yet, there's no improvement either. Another widespread disease of the redrafting stage is when the writer dreams up an event that could enrich the story. Then when he tries to insert it, he discovers that he has to change the whole story to make that event logically fit in. And yes, he starts again. Another rewriting problem is when a writer reverts to an earlier draft and tries to cram his newer material into it until he can't tell what works and what doesn't.

And we thought that writing the first draft was hard!

The main cause for all rewriting problems is not knowing what to change and what to keep from earlier drafts. The obvious solution is to identify what's working and what's not, recognize and isolate the flaws of the story before the rewrite, and then start the new draft.

But how can we identify those flaws? How can we know what works and what doesn't?

Personally, I use Dramatica (of course) to identify them. I also go through this checklist:

- *Determine if the rewrite is necessary.*

- *Determine if the rewrite should change the structure.*

- *Determine if the rewrite should change the representation.*

- *Determine if the rewrite should change the narrative drive.*

Here's how I go through every point:

Determine if the rewrite is necessary

This may seem obvious, but it's not. Insecurity is the conjoined twin of creativity, and many times producers, directors and writers find themselves wondering if the story is good enough or if a rewrite is necessary. There are ways to discover it. A "Focus Group" is an expensive but effective tool to find out. A Writer's Group is a cheaper (and sometimes even more effective) tool to evaluate the story's condition. Between these two are several alternatives, from Professional Story Analysis, to reading the story out loud to a group of teenagers just to see if it grabs their volatile attention. Whichever way we may choose, the point is to:

1. Get a feeling of how the story plays to an audience. If the audience reacts enthusiastically to it, chances are that a rewrite could do more harm than good to it, and thus, an additional draft may be inadvisable.

2. Clearly identify the parts that are not working (for example, scenes where audience interest decays, events that are too predictable, inconsistent or implausible characters...). If these parts exist, and if they're enough to produce an overall response of boredom and confusion to the story, then a rewrite is necessary.

The comments and criticisms you receive about the story help to clarify the nature of the flawed parts. You can also identify the story's rough spots by using Dramatica to see if the problem is in the Storyforming, Storyencoding, or Storyweaving. This is easy and straightforward. We do it with the next step on the checklist:

Determine if the rewrite requires changing the story's structure

A story with flawed structure—one that needs changes in its storyform or a better execution of its storyform—usually gets criticisms such as these:

- The story is disjointed.

- The story is implausible.

- The plot has too many holes.

- The story is too shallow.

- The end feels unsatisfying.

Besides having a flawed structure, there are other reasons to reevaluate the storyform of a script, such as:

- The audience finds the sad ending is too depressing and would like to see a happier one.

- The producer would want to see the Main Character as being right all along at the end of the picture.

These reasons have to do with aesthetic decisions rather than faults within the structure, but are equally influential in making a decision to rewrite. Reworking the script to allow for audience and producer expectations might produce a version that is better accepted by the audience and more positively impacts the box office.

Whatever the reason may be to change the story's structure, we open the Dramatica software, analyze the existing draft, and try to get a single storyform for it.

The key here is to find a storyform that includes most of the parts that work (those that did not get complaints, or received praise from our target audience), while leaving aside the parts that don't (the inconsistent events or characters). This is usually done through trial and error. In the end, compromises must be made. Some of our "good scenes" will have to be left out for believability, thoroughness, depth, and audience satisfaction. Don't worry—these missing scenes can be replaced with even better ones now that we have a solid structure.

Determine if the rewrite should change the storytelling

After we find the perfect structure for our story, we must check if the items that represent it (the settings, events, characters, their behavior and the dialogue wording) are satisfactory or inadequate. Here are some examples of how the audience identifies poor storytelling:

- I don't care about these characters.

- The places where it happens are too unfamiliar—I can't relate.

- I have the feeling I've seen this already.

- I expected something more original.

- This is supposed to be an *Action Film* (or a *Thriller*, or a *Comedy*)?

Some of the remarks suggest the audience doesn't connect with the storytelling used, or that they have negative associations with them and hate them from the beginning. Others say the audience is too familiar with the illustrations and sees them as clichéd and tiresome. Still other remarks plainly suggest the illustrations don't match the chosen genre.

Anyway, the process to rewrite illustrations is to:

- **Identify the structure and isolate it from the faulty storytelling**. First we find the storyform. Then we determine the Characters' construction by using the Build Characters' chart of character elements to identify missing character functions. Then map those *holes* to character who don't yet have a function. Having done that we can change the illustrations without the problem of losing coherency or consistency.

- **Write several illustrations for each of the structure points**. From these several illustrations find one that best fits the intended audience. The idea is to present several choices to the target audience and let them decide which works best. For example, write five examples for a "Goal of Obtaining" that fits the story and create three characters—with identical elements—to substitute for a character who was rejected by the audience.

Rewriting illustrations is a lot of work, but its value will be felt at the box office.

Determine if the rewrite should change the narrative drive

We now have a sound structure, and we've found some wonderful, vibrant illustrations to represent it. But have we chosen the best way to present the story to the audience? Here are some symptoms of a good story that unfolds badly:

- I saw that event coming from a mile away.

- The story lost me.

- The story is too repetitive or monotonous.

- Needs more twists and turns.

- It has so many twists and turns that it gets confusing after the first half hour.

Changing the way a story unfolds—rewriting the narrative drive—is hard. This is because finding a good way to present a story to the audience is a matter of "feeling" and experience. Each screenwriter develops his own narrative style which eventually becomes a trademark of that particular author.

Dramatica can help, though, by fixing the structure and breaking the storytelling elements into tiny parts that we can order and reorder, emphasize and de-emphasize, expose and hide until we find the perfect combination that reveals the story to the audience.

This is usually the lengthiest part of the rewriting process, but it's fun. This is especially true when we have a solid guide to the story's illustrations and structure. Event orders can change and words can be rearranged, but as long as we have a sound structural story, all the changes can improve the story.

Remember the main rule of rewriting:

> **REDRAFT ALL YOU WANT AS LONG AS IT MAKES THE STORY BETTER.**

When we're writing version after version just to appease an insecure conscience, we're just wasting our talent—or worse, ruining an otherwise good screenplay. It's best to print the script, put some brass fasteners in it, pick up the phone and call the agent to tell him, "I'm coming over. I've finished the screenplay."

EPILOGUE

All that you've read in this book—all the examples, all the exercises, all the knowledge and understanding I have about Dramatica—was accomplished by writing as many stories as I could with Dramatica.

In the end, the best advice I can give is this:

Write.

Write a lot.

I use Dramatica when I feel it's helping me and I leave it behind when I feel I'm better flying solo. I don't think of it as an authoritative guru that *validates* or *invalidates* my stories. I think of it as the tool that I use to create the story I want.

Enough said. Start writing.

APPENDICES

APPENDIX A

TWELVE QUESTIONS TO ASK ABOUT YOUR STORIES WHEN USING DRAMATICA

For the beginner (and sometimes for the expert as well), Dramatica can be quite puzzling: It uses dense, tough terms to describe your story and leaves it up to you to translate them into entertaining, appealing parts of your screenplay.

I find that the best way to turn those cold *appreciations* or *story points* into actual writing is to ask the right questions. What you need is a brainteaser, a puzzle, a riddle whose answer sparks your creative fires and shows you how those intricate story points hide the key to a compelling and delightful screenplay.

Here are the questions that help me break through the Dramatica puzzle.

1. What Is This In My Story?

Most times, I approach Dramatica with a draft already written, or at least some ideas I'd like to go into my story. Typically, an idea of mine might look something like this:

"Hanna has spent most of her life trying to win the lottery."

So, to work my story with Dramatica, I have to make that paragraph fit into a *storyform*, the underlying structure and dynamics of the story. I do this by asking myself: *"What is this? What Dramatica term represents this paragraph? What would be its function? What would be its place in the storyform?"*

For example, the above paragraph could be the Story Goal of Obtaining (*"The goal is to actually win the lottery"*). That could give me a **Lottery Caper** kind of a story, with everyone scheming how to manipulate the lottery draw.

But alternatively, the lottery could be the Main Character's Concern of Contemplation (*"Hanna constantly thinks of how it would be to win the lottery, but never even buys a ticket"*). This version could be an account of a woman who obsesses about the lottery in order to escape her reality—a much more dramatic tale.

The lottery could also be the Impact Character's Issue of Dream (*"Hanna's pipe dreams of winning the lottery deeply impact the Main Character's attitude"*). This could make a story with a nutty, dreaming character who turns out to have the right outlook in the end.

Or the lottery could be the Subjective Story's Problem of Speculation (*"Hanna and the other major character fight constantly about her implausible expectations of winning the lottery"*). This option could give me a story about how aspirations can tear apart a relationship.

Each choice will make that initial paragraph work in a different way. But also, as a whole, each option gives me a different story. So I have to be really sure of which kind of movie I want to write.

I work this question by trying several answers, entering each into the software and watching how the storyform transforms until it gives me the story I like best. It's also helpful to give myself some time to ponder which kind of story I want.

2. What Are My Story Priorities?

In Dramatica, every decision you make affects the rest of the story, and very often you have two or more incompatible choices you'd like to fit into the same Storyform. At times like this I ask myself: *"What Are My Story Priorities?"*

Is my story plot-oriented (like most **Action** or **Mystery** movies)? *Or is it character-oriented* (like most **Dramas**)? *Which are the more important points in my genre?* For example, in most **Romance** and **Buddy Pictures**, the Subjective Story Throughline is a priority. In most **Sci-Fi** movies, the Environment—Situation as the Overall Story Domain—is basic.

Which are my best-drafted scenes? Which paragraphs of my draft can I do without? These questions help me make choices and get the Storyform I want.

Now, I have to remind myself that in Dramatica there's no such thing as "the *right* storyform." No structure is inherently "better" than another. It's just that I'd be happier with a particular storyform, and it would be easier writing my story within one particular structure than with any other. It's all a matter of personal choice.

When I work with the above questions, I first make sure I understand the meaning of the given story points (*I encode them to make sure of my comprehension*), and that I have a good grasp of the Storyform (*I write a short synopsis from the encoded story points*).

Then I *map* all the possible choices on a sheet of paper, and give each one some "points" in regard to genre relevance, audience preference, and my own personal liking. I add the points up, and that gives me a clear idea of my final decision.

Of course when setting priorities, I have to be ruthless and ready to throw away any material I've previously written that doesn't fit my final choice. It's hard, I know, but hard decisions are what writing is all about. (If you can't bear to let them go, you can put them in an "orphaned ideas" folder for use in some other story.)

3. Why Is Dramatica Giving Me This?

How many times have you made a choice about a character only to find out the software has automatically selected a perplexing direction for your plot based on your random character choice?

Dramatica is the only story development software that automatically sets other items based on your own choices. But many times these may seem oddly selected, baffling, and/or creatively constraining. That's when it's time to ask yourself: *"Why is Dramatica giving me this particular suggestion?"*

The point here is not to try to understand the inner workings of the software, but to look for the creative possibilities within the given story point.

Each Dramatica point is structured to increase the conflict, to take it to every story level (internal, external, and universal), and to make it reach all the characters. So, when the software confronts you with a puzzling story point (e.g., *Why are Impulsive Responses the Consequence of not achieving the Goal of Progress?*), try to think of its dramatic and creative possibilities!

Ask yourself these questions:

- **How does this story point increase the conflict?** For example, Progress and Impulsive Responses are items of different natures. When the Consequence is contradictory in nature to the Goal, will penalize the characters if they fail to achieve the Goal – thereby automatically increasing the story's stakes.

- **Which level of conflict do I reach with this story point?** For example, Progress is external in nature, while Impulsive Responses are internal. For the characters, this means that failing to make progress toward the Goal will not only deteriorate the situation, but will also negatively affect their psyches.

- **Which characters would be in most conflict with this story point?** For example, Progress implies a change, while Impulsive Responses are hard to alter. This means that, while some characters may be good in dealing with a changing situation, they won't be good in dealing with a static one; therefore, they will be more vulnerable to the consequence.

And always ask yourself:

- **How can I get the most story advantage out of this?** For example, now that I have all these elements, what horrible, devastating reactions based on Impulsive Responses can I create for my characters if they don't achieve the Goal?

When I work with this question, I write the story point on a piece of paper and, below it, all its dramatic possibilities: *Which level of conflict is it affecting most? What are its consequences? What could be its causes?*

Then I try to visualize my characters and how it affects them: *Which character is in conflict with it? Who is pleased by it? What is the reaction of each character to it?* Out of this often comes a clear idea of how I can use the story point creatively, how I can use it to improve my story, and why Dramatica suggested it to me.

4. Why Have I Chosen This?

This may seem obvious, but it's not always. Lots of times I make choices in the software but, when trying later to incorporate those choices into my script, I'm baffled by them.

This sometimes happens because my Dramatica-using decisions are made almost by instinct, by a little voice in the back of my head that tells me how my plot should develop and how my characters should behave. For example, I see the element "Self-Aware" and instinctively think of "selfish"; I even recall an ex-girlfriend who inspired me to think of that character trait.

By no means should you extinguish that voice in the back of your head. In fact, jot down on a pad whatever it tells you (e.g., *"This character's self-awareness takes her to the point of selfishness. Remember Zelda, that wench . . ."*). Write down the reasons for your conclusions, and keep a record of your changes in the Storyform. This is a wonderful way to develop your story, and to understand the deeper intricacies of Dramatica.

5. What Does This MEAN?

If you're like me, you may read a Dramatica story point over and over, and still not grasp its meaning, right? That's because a story point (e.g., *"Inaction as the Subjective Story Symptom"*) consists of two parts: The Term (Inaction) and the Function ("The Subjective Story Symptom"). And the only way to understand it all is to figure out how the particular Term works in that particular Function.

Here's what I do: First I look at the Term definition in the Dramatica Dictionary ("Inaction: Intentionally taking no action"). Then I look for the Function definition in the "Explanation" screen of the Query System ("Subjective Story Symptom: The principal symptom of the difficulties between the Main and Impact Characters"). Then I write a paragraph that blends both definitions, such as:

- *"The Main Character and Impact Character take no action to stop the symptoms of the difficulties between them. . ."* – OR –

- *"As a symptom of the difficulties between the Main Character and Impact Character, they intentionally take no action..."* – OR –

- *"No one's taking action until the Main Character and Impact Character resolve the difficulties between them..."*

I write several possible combinations of those definitions until I find one that clicks for me, suits my story, and provides me with ideas for telling it – one that makes me understand that particular story point.

6. What Does This Have To Do With My Story?

This is not a gripe, but a legitimate question. *Where do these cryptic story points belong in my story? What forms should they take and how could they fit into my storytelling?* You get the answers by using a process of free association:

On a piece of paper, jot down your story subject (e.g., "Divorce ...") and then scribble around it every related word that you can think of (e.g., "Lawyers, Arguments, Alimony, Infidelity, Drunkenness...") – whatever comes to mind.

Then, on another piece of paper, note the Dramatica term and its context (e.g., *Test* as the *Overall Story Problem*). Now write what that could mean, such as, "Any instance where a Test can cause a problem for everybody." Then free your mind and think of whatever examples you can of the term in its context, instances where a test can cause a problem for everybody: DNA Tests, HIV Tests, Lie Detector Tests, and Sobriety Tests come to mind.

Sooner or later, you'll find at least a couple of related items are on both lists – there's your storytelling. Congratulations, you've found a precise encoding by matching free associations!

7. How Does This Fit Within My Story?

Dramatica aims to make sure that any story point the software gives you fits coherently within your story. Therefore this question is aimed to help you find coherent storytelling for whatever Dramatica gives you.

Suppose your story subject is about a *Dysfunctional Family*. That is your world, your total, the whole that you're going to divide to find each term. So do some research on your subject, and write down on a note pad whatever you've found.

Let's start by finding your Domain (e.g., *Activities*). Look at your research notes and <u>underline</u> whatever has to do with your Domain (e.g., the *Activities* of a Dysfunctional Family: *Violent Arguments, Verbal Abuse, Brawling, Heavy Drinking, Drug Use, Unexplained Absences* ...). Write the underlined phrases on a separate piece of paper.

To find examples for your Concern (e.g., *Understanding*), check this new piece of paper and <u>underline</u> all items that have to do with your Concern. For example, underline the Activities/Efforts to Understand – or, in our Dysfunctional Family's case, the Activities that *keep them from* Understanding one another. For example, the *Violent Arguments*, the *Verbal Abuse*, and the *Unexplained Absences*. Then write those on yet another piece of paper.

To get illustrations for your Issue (e.g., *Conditioning*), read the preceding Concern paper and <u>underline</u> only the items that have to do with the Issue (e.g., underline the *Conditioned* Activities that keep the family members from Understanding each other: the *Violent Arguments* and the *Verbal Abuse*). Then copy these onto their own Issue sheet.

And finally, to get illustrations for your Story Problem (e.g. *Inertia* – a tendency to continue), take the Issue sheet and <u>underline</u> any items having to do with the designated Problem (e.g., underline the *Continued* Activities that Conditioned the family members into not being able to Understand each other, such as the *Verbal Abuse*).

See? Here's a way to find your entire encoding by simply underlining and copying. And as might be obvious, the greater your research, the better your encoding will be.

This one was kind of fun, wasn't it?

8. To What Extent Can I Take This?

Answering this question helps for writing as well as for understanding any obscure Dramatica story point.

First, start by thinking and writing down some encoding for a specific story point (e.g., "Impulsive Responses as the Story Goal"). It doesn't have to be great encoding, or even good encoding: Just write the first thing that pops into your mind (e.g., "Their Goal is to take control of their Impulsive Responses").

Now, think of another example that stretches the definition, an illustration that takes the story point to its limits, combining both term and function in a way that's not necessarily Dramatica-kosher. For example:

- *"Their Impulsive Responses keep them from achieving any Goal..."*
  – OR –

- *"They'll know they've reached their Goal by their Impulsive Responses..."*
  – OR –

- *"Their goal is to make a list of all the possible Impulsive Responses."*

It doesn't matter if you break the rules, ignore the definition, or end up far from it. The idea here is to take the story point to its limit. For example:

- *"They have weird Impulsive Responses when they see someone accomplishing a Goal."*

- *"They think achieving a Goal is a matter of Impulsive Responses."*

- *"When they see a hockey Goalie, they have the Impulsive Response to punch him."*

After finding several examples, put them in an ordered list that goes from the most conventional to the most far-fetched. Then draw a line where you think the story point limit is, where you believe Dramatica ends and "THE TWILIGHT ZONE" begins.

Think of the encoding for your story. Should it be:

- Well within "the Dramatica conventions"?

- Far out in "outer space"?

- Right at "the borderline"?

Every time I do this exercise, I find Dramatica terms and functions can be stretched further. I'm now convinced that the most unconventional and bizarre stories could have been written with Dramatica, assuming the writer had enough imagination. I like this exercise. I believe stretching a concept makes the difference between following orders and being creative.

9. What's This Scene All About?

In an already written draft, how do you know which scenes to keep and which scenes to remove ? How can you decide, if you don't know, what each scene is all about?

At the core of each scene, there should be a change, a turn, an event that makes the story take off in a new direction. It could be a revelation, a character's action, an answer to a previous question, a stroke of fortune… Whichever, it will be evident that this incident takes the story to another stage – one that couldn't have been reached without that particular scene.

Thus to find out what a scene is all about, you need to set aside all of its elements, one by one, until only this *turning event* remains.

When you have it, you can identify if your scene is primarily a Plot Scene, a Character Scene, a Thematic Scene, or a Genre Scene.

- A Plot Scene is one with a *turning event* that alters or advances the plot toward an outcome of success or failure, such as a consequential discovery, a resolution that takes the characters into a new journey, an unexpected death…

- A Character Scene is one with a *turning event* that changes the character's nature, reveals an unseen characteristic, or ultimately confirms the character's nature. For example, a matriarch sticks to her principles despite the consequences, a hero acts cowardly, a villain acts nobly…

- A Thematic Scene is one with a *turning event* that transforms or confirms the story's viewpoint or puts it to the test, such as a scene where "crime does indeed pay," or "love *doesn't* conquer all," or we see the ultimate consequence of "blood [being] thicker than water"…

- A Genre Scene is one with a *turning event* that contains elements integral to the script's genre. For example, heroic deeds in an action flick, laughs in a comedy, blood-letting in a gore film…

Once you have identified if a scene mostly serves the Plot, Character, Theme or Genre, it is easier to see which Dramatica item connects with it. Specifically:

- Plot Scenes have to do with the Signposts, the Journeys, and the Additional Overall Story (OS) Story Points (*Goal, Consequence, Dividends, Requirements, etc.*).

- Character Scenes have to do with the Character Dynamics (*Resolve, Growth, Approach, Problem-Solving Style, etc.*), and the Character-Building Elements (*Motivations, Purposes, Methodologies, Evaluations, etc.*).

- Theme Scenes have to do with the story's *Issues, Problems, Solutions, Symptoms,* and *Responses.*

- Genre Scenes have to do with the story's *Domains* and *Concerns.*

A great exercise to help you master Dramatica is to ask yourself, while watching a movie: "What's this scene all about?" First identify if it's a Plot, Character, Theme or Genre scene. Then try to connect it mentally with its respective Dramatica term. This exercise is a must for screenwriters!

10. When Can I Reveal This?

A story develops step by step, incident by incident, little by little, disclosing its secrets slowly and surprising the audience with each event. Dramatica, on the other hand, gives you all the story parts at the same time, and with little clue about which should come first.

The beginning and the conclusion, the assumed deceits and the final truths, the problems and its solutions – all appear before your eyes the minute you get a storyform.

It's then up to you to turn that glob of story ingredients into a well told story, into the amazing sequence of discoveries we all expect to see. So, you'll have to ask yourself when to reveal each story point, each incident, each detail. This is what Storyweaving is all about.

There are many ways to Storyweave, but all of them require some trial and error. So...

- See how your story turns if you reveal the questions before the answers. Then see how it feels if you reveal the answers before the questions. For example, what's more terrifying: 1) A character opening a door and discovering—along with the audience—a killer hiding on the other side of it? Or 2) letting the audience see the killer hide behind the door, then showing them each suspenseful move as the unsuspecting victim unlocks it?

- See what happens when you show the solutions before the problems. For example, show us the overlooked girl next door, then our "lonely guy" main character who's looking for true love (but isn't looking right in his own neighborhood). Or show us the treasure chest in the adventurer's attic (while he's off circling the globe to find it).

- Experiment with stories that start with the conclusion. For example, a story told by a dead guy who narrates how he was killed (SUNSET BOULEVARD). Or an average girl who suddenly wakes up in a royal bed in a palace and has to reconstruct what happened last night and how she got there.

Always ask yourself if it's too *early* to reveal something, or if it's too *late*. Sometimes, changing where you reveal a single item in a story can make the difference between a predictable bore and an engaging thrill ride. We've all seen movies that could've benefited from some item shifting, right?

11. Which Movies Are Akin To My Story?

This is very simple. Imagine that your story is already written, produced, released, and issued on DVD: In which row of the video store would you put it? Next to which movies will it be placed? Which genre will be stamped on its box?

Once you've answered these questions and are sure about them, go to the video store and rent the movies that are akin to your story.

Watch the movies and analyze them with Dramatica. Make files of those and incorporate them into your "Examples" library.

Your analysis will help you immensely in crafting your own story. Several questions you have for your screenplay – from Storyforming to Storyweaving – will be answered as you watch those movies.

You'll also find which elements are successful and which are mistakes, which are tried-and-true and should go into your story, and which are exhausted clichés that should go in the garbage can.

Other filmmakers have done half your homework for you; it's time for you to accept their contributions.

12. What Would Be A Good Question At This Moment?

In other words, "What should I ask myself that I haven't already asked?" This question is actually very helpful – not only to find which of the above questions applies to your story at any point in your creative process, but also to conceive your own brainteasers and, in time, your own system of Dramatica writing.

It's important to develop your own personal method of story development; one that works for you and provides you a happy and productive process every time.

"What would be a good question at this moment?" is, of course, both the most important query and the toughest. Sometimes you may ponder it for days before getting an answer. Other times an answer can seem to appear immediately. The answer can come out of anything.

Try this:

- Take any of the other questions in this chapter, disassemble it, and rework it in a way that helps you better (e.g., *"What Is This?"* may become *"How Does This Part Of My Story Translate To Dramatica Terms?"*).

- Do likewise with any question from the software's "Query System" (e.g., *"What Is The Goal In Your Story?"* may become *"What Is The Common Interest For All My Characters?"*).

- Use anything posted at the Dramatica site as a topic to question (e.g., try adapting the "Tip Of The Month" to work for your current story).

- Read your story notes and make questions about them.

Anything can spark a question – anything. Just as much as anything can spark its answer.

"What Would Be A Good Question At This Moment?" is the toughest query indeed… but is always worth answering.

Use these twelve questions when you feel a block in your Dramatica writing process, when you're stuck in a rut, or when you want to advance to the next level of Dramatica knowledge. You can use one, several, or all of them. They interact nicely with each other, and apply to any part of the creative process.

APPENDIX B

GENRE AND THE MAIN AND IMPACT CHARACTERS

Who are our most important Characters?

What's our movie all about?

Choosing our central characters is more than just populating our movie. These Characters hold the key to solving the plot's central problem and the standpoint from where the audience is going to watch how our story develops. By identifying our most important characters, we control what our movie is all about.

Dramatica addresses this matter with a pair of unique concepts: *The Main Character (MC)* and the *Impact Character (IC)*. These are more than fictional people. They are the inner core of our story, provide the necessary reference to understand our theme, represent essential parts of our plot, eventually define the genre, and make it possible to tell the story we want to tell.

Here's an inventory of different kinds of movies—organized by **Genre**—with a reference to their typical Main Character and Impact Character: Their personalities, relationships, traits, and other goodies help us choose the ideal Main and Impact Characters.

Love Stories

You've guessed it; in this genre, the Main and Impact Characters embody the romantic interest that develops into the amorous relationship *(Erich Segal's* LOVE STORY*)*. Choosing the lovers as Main and Impact Characters is one quality that makes this genre identifiable. If we choose another set of characters as Main Character and Impact Character, such as the boyfriend and his father-in-law, the story's emotional weight automatically shifts to that relationship and the genre is less recognizable.

Similar Genres are:

- **Romantic Comedies**. The rules apply, but the storytelling becomes humorous *(Neil Simon's* THE GOODBYE GIRL*)*.

- *The Erotica Genre.* The interest between the Main and Impact Characters is fundamentally carnal (LAST TANGO IN PARIS).

- *Buddy Pictures.* Main and Impact are just buddies (THELMA AND LOUISE). Commonly, **Buddy Pictures** pair opposite personalities, give them a task to complete, and make them buddies through the endeavor (*Walter Hill's* 48 HRS).

Horror Movies

Here it's a good idea to make the Main Character a potential victim while granting the Impact Character the role of scary villain (*Wes Craven's* A NIGHTMARE ON ELM STREET). For many stories, the antagonist is not combined with the Impact Character. But, in the *Horror* genre the Impact/Villain combination gives us a terrifying foe that's bigger than life, and that's what this genre is all about.

This applies for all *Horror* subgenres: *Supernatural* (POLTERGEIST), *Uncanny* (THE FLY), *Slasher* (HALLOWEEN), *Gore* (THE TEXAS CHAINSAW MASSACRE), *Gothic* (CANDYMAN). The possible exception to this rule is the *Black Comedy/Horror Parody* (SCARY MOVIE) which needs a ridiculous villain, and is not as effective when the Impact Character is also the villain.

Action/Adventure Stories

Like the *Horror* genre, these films need a huge Arch-Villain that seems invincible and wreaks mayhem at all levels. To do this, give the villain character an atrocious set of evil powers (the *Android* in THE TERMINATOR), and leave the Main and Impact roles for some other Characters (Sarah Connor and Kyle Reese). However, when the villain also has the function of Impact Character (*Darth Vader* in THE EMPIRE STRIKES BACK), he becomes fully developed and completely evil. His reach pervades the emotional core of the story and he develops to be a colossal, legendary adversary.

The Main Character in these stories is usually a Hero with special skills which makes him the only one who could deal with the villain (*Luke Skywalker* in STAR WARS). Even then, he must go through a change and develop extra skills to defeat this terrible enemy.

Related to this genre are:

- *Spy Films.* The same as the *Action/Adventure* genre—skillful heroes and dreadful villains (GOLDFINGER). Some *Spy/Mysteries* reveal the real villain only at the end (THE SPY WHO CAME IN FROM THE COLD). While consistently functioning throughout the story as Impact

Character, the dreadful villain exposes his true villainous nature only at the final showdown.

- **Disaster Movies**. Most of them have a love interest as the Impact Character (like in TITANIC), and that puts the cataclysm story in the emotional background. However, since the disaster itself is the villain in this genre, these stories benefit from developing the devastation as the Impact Character Throughline (THE POSEIDON ADVENTURE). It is tricky to write a story like this, but the results are appealing.

Road Movies

In most **Road Movies** the Main Character is an unrelenting traveler *(Mad Max* in THE ROAD WARRIOR) while the Impact Character is the fundamental reason for those travels (the *Town-Refinery People* in that movie). Many times, the justification for those travels is found at the traveler's destination (NURSE BETTY). At other times we identify the explanation for the trip at the point of departure (JEEPERS CREEPERS), or when the Impact Character chases the Main Character throughout the picture *(Steven Spielberg's* DUEL).

More frequent is the **Road/Buddy Picture**, where Main and Impact Characters play the most incompatible couple, forced to travel together (PLANES, TRAINS AND AUTOMOBILES; MIDNIGHT RUN).

Crime Movies

These stories rely on a puzzling and surprising progression of events, so usually a *red herring* is used as one of the major characters. A red herring is a distraction or false clue that keeps the characters and audience from finding the final truth.

Its application in specific genres usually go like this:

- **Caper Stories**. The Main Character is a criminal mastermind *(Danny Ocean* in OCEAN'S ELEVEN), while the Impact Character is a distraction that keeps him from completing the heist *(Tess Ocean,* OCEAN'S ELEVEN).

- **Mysteries** and **Whodunits**. The Main Character has the role of crime solver, whereas the Impact Character represents a false clue about the crime and represents a grave danger for the Main Character (VERTIGO).

- **Detective Stories**. The Main Character is a professional crime solver. The Impact Character starts as a mere distraction and grows to be a severe menace (THE MALTESE FALCON).

- *Suspense Movies* and **Thrillers**. The key to these genres is making the Main Character an appealing, potential victim. The Impact Character is more often a distraction that increases the victim's risk (REAR WINDOW).

- *Police Stories*. Most of them are gritty **Action** movies, **Whodunits**, or **Social Dramas** where the Main and Impact Characters are both cops with opposite views on law enforcement issues (TRAINING DAY).

- *Prison Movies*. Like the **Police Stories**, these are different kinds of films where the central characters are inmates in a correctional institution and have different approaches on how to deal with their confinement (PAPILLON).

Social Dramas

These stories focus on a social problem and give the central characters opposite perspectives about it—typically from both ends of the problem's spectrum. Particular genres are:

- *Modern Epics*. The ordinary person battles the establishment. The Main Character is that Everyday Joe, while City Hall stands for the Impact Character (MR. SMITH GOES TO WASHINGTON).

- *Classroom Dramas*. Main and Impact Characters are typically teacher and student (LEAN ON ME).

- *Courtroom Dramas*. A classic pairing makes the Main Character an attorney and the Impact Character his defendant (PRIMAL FEAR).

- *Psycho Dramas*. Emotional stories that deal with treating mental illness. Usually the Main Character is the doctor and the Impact his patient (AWAKENINGS).

- *Domestic Dramas*. Problems about dysfunctional families and abusive relationships. Commonly, the Main and Impact Characters are spouses (WHOSE AFRAID OF VIRGINIA WOOLF?), or parent and child (KRAMER VS. KRAMER).

- *Business Dramas*. These take place at the office of a prosperous commercial firm and deal with the problems of today's materialistic society. Usually the Main and Impact Characters are businesspersons in similar conditions, with shared concerns, equal goals, but opposite attitudes (WALL STREET).

- **Holocaust Dramas**. The Main and Impact Characters share similar conditions but have different perspectives (CONSPIRACY).

Personal Dramas

Film critics, such as Norman Friedman, and Studio executives have recently developed a series of genres based on *character arc*. For example, a story starts with a character being his usual self, then *stuff* happens to him, and he ends up changed. Now, I define the genre according to *how* that usual self starts out, *what* stuff happens, and *how* he is changed.

I call these genres **Personal Dramas**. Here's how studio execs categorize each one of them:

- **Education Plot**. The character starts with a pessimistic view of the world, goes through a learning process of sorts, and ends with a more optimistic outlook. Generally speaking, the one that changes is the Main Character, and the Impact Character is the one that teaches him this new world vision (THE PRINCE OF TIDES).

- **Disillusionment Plot**. The character starts with a hopeful—yet naïve— notion of life, receives a misguided education in the ways of the world, and winds up bitter and alone. The naïve one is the Main Character, while the bogus teacher is the Impact Character (THE GREAT GATSBY).

- **Redemption Plot**. The character starts by wronging himself and others, goes through a series of experiences that make him see the light, and then redeems himself by doing the right thing. This saved character should be the Main Character, while the Impact Character is the one that shows him the light (SCHINDLER'S LIST).

- **Punitive Plot**. The character starts doing the right thing, but quickly changes and starts harming everybody around him. He won't change back, so he's destroyed—or seriously punished—in the end. The Main Character is the one who goes bad and thus is destroyed. The Impact Character tries unsuccessfully to make him come back to his senses (FALLING DOWN).

- **Testing Plot**. This is about a tenacious character that goes through a series of trials to prove his unbreakable will. The Main Character is the

unbreakable one, while the Impact Character is the tormentor that puts
him to the test (MEN OF HONOR).

Children Genres

Admit it or not, children love to learn. The world is so new to them and so full
of discoveries that they imagine it as an unending learning experience. The Main
Characters in most children stories lack experience and are like fish out of water,
while the Impact Characters have experience, and become instructor-like friends
who take them firmly in hand through the adventurous brave new world.

The basic difference in characters for *Children Genres* is in the target
audience. In the *Family Appeal Movies*, the teaching character is conventional and
of traditional values (IT'S A WONDERFUL LIFE). In *Children/Juvenile Movies*, the
teacher is exceptionally unconventional, and so are the values he teaches (SHREK).

In a related genre, the central characters of the *Coming-of-Age Story* are
reluctant to give or receive the education that revolves around the core of the story.
The events must come to a painful, traumatic point to let the lessons begin (THE
LION KING).

Until now, all the genres we've reviewed have specific structures and, therefore,
have typical Main and Impact Characters, but some genres are defined by story items
other than their structure.

Here are some of them:

Genres Of Particular Backdrop

These are movies classified by the place, historical age or variety of activities
that characterize them. They include: *Westerns*, *Science Fiction Stories*, *Fantasy
Stories*, *War Films*, *Sport Films* and *Historical Pieces*. Apart from their particular
environment, their structures are the same as those of *Action Films* (THE MATRIX),
of *Epics* (1984) or of some types of *Dramas* (RAGING BULL). The Main/Impact
Character rules of the structural genres apply.

Genres Of Particular Storytelling Style

Other movies rely on their manner of expression—the tone in which the story is
told or the elements are used to tell it. These include all kinds of *Comedies*: *Broad
Comedies*, *Situation Comedies*, *Fantastic Comedies*, *Farces*, *Parodies*, *and
Satires*; and *Musicals*: *Musical Comedy*, *Musical Drama*, and *Rock-Opera*.

The key here is to recognize that any genre can be told with any particular
storytelling. A *Comedy* can take the structure of an *Action Story* (THE BLUES

BROTHERS; TEAM AMERICA!), of a **Detective Story** (NAKED GUN, FROM THE FILES OF POLICE SQUAD), or of an **Education Plot** (DOWN AND OUT IN BEVERLY HILLS).

Also, any genre can be told with **Musical** elements—MOULIN ROUGE! (a **Love Story** structure), DANCER IN THE DARK (**Testing Plot** structure), or CABARET (**Social Drama** structure).

This freedom of form is the biggest difficulty in these genres. Since we don't have a particular structure to define our story, we have to be pretty funny, incredibly flashy, or have fantastically catchy music to make a good movie.

Reality Genres

Some stories are strictly based on real facts—**Documentaries**, **Docudramas**, and **Biography Movies** among them.

Though exposing the "bare facts" is the norm in these genres, the audience enjoys them more when we arrange the facts within the structure of a particular genre. For example, ROGER AND ME has a **Modern Epic** structure; WACO, THE RULES OF ENGAGEMENT has a **Social Drama** structure.

We need structure to create emotions in the viewer. Putting emotion in these **Reality Genres** clarifies the exposed "bare facts" and makes them more enjoyable.

We've covered enough genres to get us started and enable us to choose our Main and Impact Characters.

Keep in mind the references listed here are as basic as it gets. Every genre makes exceptions to these rules and reinvents itself with each movie written.

The key—as always—is to view and analyze as many films as we can. Define your genre, watch every picture in it, make notes about the central characters, and get to know what is trite and what isn't. The more you know, the better your script will be, and the better chance you'll have to sell it.

APPENDIX C
GENRE AND THE DRAMATICA DOMAINS

Where should we set our story?

Again—what's our movie all about?

Setting isn't just the place where our tale happens, nor its time, space, length, and historical period. Setting goes far beyond time and space. It has little to do with background and scenery. It's much deeper than that. Setting is the source of the story's conflict.

Let me explain. On a shallow level, setting is just the time and place of our story. So for the audience, a **Western** is any tale in the 1800s American frontier, and whatever happens in space must be **Sci-Fi**. But, on a deeper level—for the screenwriter—time and space embrace the characters' problems. Location brings about specific evils. And the story's troubles have to be consistent with the particular surroundings. For example, if I try to set a **Light Romantic Comedy** in the middle of D-Day at Normandy, my characters will have a hard time romancing one another and may only care about saving their lives. Conversely, if my characters are average farmers set in average farmland, there is little conflict, and my story becomes the ultimate snoozefest.

To straighten out these setting/structure issues, Dramatica has set up the *Domains*: These are specific areas where particular lines of our story are set. They assure coherence within structure and setting; consistent time, place, and events; and build up enough conflict to write a great story.

Dramatica has four different Domains: Conflicting *Situations,* challenging *Activities*, troublesome *Fixed Ideas,* and problematic *Ways Of Thinking and Manipulations*. Depending on our decisions, Dramatica assigns each to a different story thread.

So, how can we decide which Domain works best for our particular story? Let's see which style of story we're writing to make our choice.

Genres Set In A Situation

These are movies defined by the circumstances surrounding the characters. The *Situation Domain* best defines these genres. Each of the following genres use a situation in a particular way:

Horror Stories

The *Situation Domain* is a terrifying environment that ensnares all the characters—so it's used mostly as the *Overall Story Domain*.

In **Supernatural Horror** *(*THE HAUNTING*)*, the environment has no logical explanation. In an **Uncanny Story** *(*ALIEN*)*, the situation is logical but still holds the characters in shocking circumstances. And in a **Hybrid Super-Uncanny Horror** *(*THE SHINING*)*, the situation's nature is never clear.

Variants include the **Gothic Story** *(*FROM HELL*)*, where the dark circumstances only beset the Main Character—thus, it is the *Main Character Domain*. And the **Black Comedy** *(*ONCE BITTEN*)*—where only one character steps into the not-so-scary situation like a fish out of water—so it's also the *Main Character Domain*.

Disaster Movies

A catastrophe traps all the characters *(*EARTHQUAKE*)*, therefore *Situation* is the *Domain* of the *Overall Story*.

Road/Buddy Picture

Two characters are forced into the road cosmos *(*THELMA AND LOUISE*)*. This *Situation* is the *Domain* of the *Subjective (*Main vs. Impact*) Story*.

Police Stories

These explore the law-enforcement microcosmos *(*SERPICO*)*. *Situation* is the *Overall Story Domain*.

Prison Movies

The jail world becomes the *Situation* for the *Overall Story* *(*MIDNIGHT EXPRESS*)*.

Genres Set In Activities

If the audience's attention is keen on the characters' activities, our primary interest should be about the *Activities* (Physics) *Domain.* Here are the related genres and how to use it:

Action/Adventure Stories

Spectacular doings are the norm in these stories (RAIDERS OF THE LOST ARK). These feats encompass all the characters, so this requires an *Overall Story Domain* of *Activities.* The **Action/Adventure** structure is also the basis for several other genres:

- **Westerns** (THE MAGNIFICENT SEVEN) are **Action Stories** that happen to take place in the frontier.

- **Science Fiction Stories** (STAR WARS) are **Action Stories** placed in space or in virtual realities.

- **Fantasy Stories** (THE LORD OF THE RINGS) are **Action Stories** situated in a fantastic world.

- **War Films** (THE BRIDGE ON THE RIVER KWAI) are **Adventure Stories** set in a battle.

- **Spy Films** (XXX *starring Vin Diesel*) are **Action Films** surrounding a super agent.

No secrets here.

Road Movies

Unlike the *Situation Domain* of the **Road/Buddy Pictures**, **Road Movies** focus on intensive Actions that affect all the characters (MAD MAX); these require an *Overall Story Domain* of *Activities.*

Buddy Pictures

These are also different from the **Road/Buddy Picture**. Here the action affects principally the Main and Impact Characters (DIRTY ROTTEN SCOUNDRELS), and the *Activities Domain* is applied to the Subjective Story.

Crime Movies

Crime is an activity, and thus, **Crime Movies** are defined by the characters' proceedings (GOODFELLAS). As a rule, the Overall Story has the *Activities Domain* here. This applies to nearly all its subgenres:

- **Caper Story** (THE HOT ROCK), where a big heist marks the activity.

- *Detective Story* (THE BIG SLEEP), where the activities either are made by the detective or made to stop him.

- *Suspense Movie* or *Thriller* (NORTH BY NORTHWEST), where the actions involve the intent to kill or avoid being killed.

Romantic Comedies

Unlike other sorts of *Love Stories*, *Romantic Comedies* are defined by the hilarious courtship actions (SHE'S ALL THAT), thus the *Main and Impact relationship* (Subjective Story Throughline) has an *Activities Domain*.

Social Dramas

Some *Social Dramas* are also characterized by their specific activities:

- The *Modern Epic* (VIVA ZAPATA!) is typified by the ordinary person's actions against the powers that be, and uses a *Main Character Domain* of *Activities*.

- Most *Domestic Dramas* (WHAT'S LOVE GOT TO DO WITH IT?) depict couple relationships based on violence, and employ a *Subjective Story Domain* of *Activities*.

Personal Dramas

Similarly, some *Personal Dramas* are recognized by the characters' activities:

- The *Punitive Plot* involves the reproachable actions of the leading role (FALLING DOWN) and has a *Main Character Domain* of *Activities*.

- The *Testing Plot* is the conflicting character's actions that make the tests (COOL HAND LUKE), and it uses an *Impact Character Domain* of *Activities*.

Genres Set In Fixed Attitudes

The conflict in these movies grows from the characters' dispositions and their biases toward the items discussed. The *Fixed Attitude* (Mind) *Domain* is obviously the basic choice here. The particular genres are:

Social Dramas

From GET ON THE BUS to THE GREEN MILE, most **Social Dramas** center on prejudices or intransigent social attitudes. Typically, the *Overall Story* is the one under the *Fixed Attitudes Domain*. This exists in all these specific genres:

- **Classroom Dramas** (*Spike Lee's* SCHOOL DAZE).

- **Courtroom Dramas** (TO KILL A MOCKINGBIRD).

- **Psycho Dramas** (FRANCES).

- **Business Dramas** (WALL STREET).

- **Holocaust Dramas** (SOPHIE'S CHOICE).

Love Stories

The most difficult problem in a **Love Story** is keeping the lovers apart. Since the movie will end when the couple is finally together, how can the writer separate two sweethearts for nearly the entire film? Prejudices are a good way to keep them apart (ABOUT LAST NIGHT), and an *Overall Story Domain* of *Fixed Attitudes* is the way to go.

The Erotica Genre

Unlike porn (which is mainly activities—or, only activities), **Erotica** is defined by a mental obsession (LADY CHATTERLEY'S LOVER) and an *Overall Story Domain* of *Fixed Attitudes*.

Genres Based In Manipulations And Manners Of Thinking

The trick here is realizing that some of these movies deal with the characters' manipulations, as **Personal Dramas** do, while others manipulate the audience's perception, like most **Mysteries**. Either way, they take advantage of the *Manipulation* (Psychology) *Domain* and its effect. Here are the particular genres:

Mysteries and Whodunits

From THE USUAL SUSPECTS to WILD THINGS, these pictures are the typical example of how to use a *Manipulation Overall Story Domain* to deceive the viewers and to create many surprising twists.

Personal Dramas

On the other hand, most **Personal Dramas** use the same *Overall Story Domain* of *Manipulation* to show deep and complicated character evolution. From LOLITA to TENDER MERCIES, these films work by revealing the character's way of thinking and its painful development. Specific applications are:

- The **Education Plot**. The *Overall Story* manipulates the central character attitude from bad to good (AMERICAN BEAUTY).

- The **Disillusionment Plot**. The *Overall Story* turns the central character outlook from good to bad (WELCOME TO THE DOLLHOUSE).

- The **Redemption Plot**, where the central character's saving deeds makes a change in the *Overall Story* (AMERICAN HISTORY X).

Coming of Age Stories

Growing up means changing your way of thinking (REBEL WITHOUT A CAUSE). Usually this change affects everyone in this genre, so the *Manipulation Domain* covers the *Overall Story*.

Settings In Comedy

Comedy depends mostly on the storytelling, yet still *Comedy* subgenres are emphasized by an apt use of Dramatica Domains:

- A *Situation Comedy* (SOME LIKE IT HOT) lets the jokes originate from awkward situations. This works well with an *Overall Story Domain* of *Situation*.

- A *Physical Comedy* (BLAZING SADDLES) is based on the characters' hilarious actions. This needs an *Activities Overall Story Domain*.

- A *Comedy Of Attitudes or Manners* (DR. STRANGELOVE OR: HOW I LEARNED TO STOP WORRYING AND LOVE THE BOMB) is centered on the characters' fixed ideas and obsessions. This uses an *Overall Story Domain* of *Fixed Attitudes*.

- A *Comedy Of Thoughts or Errors* (HANNA AND HER SISTERS) springs from funny mental confusions and humorous manipulations. This has an *Overall Story Domain* of *Manipulation*.

One of the key ingredients of *Comedy* is exaggeration, but what should we exaggerate—the situation, the actions, the ideas, or the thoughts? Understanding our subgenre and Domain will make clear where our funny stuff should come from.

Genres Without A Specific Setting

Other kinds of movies have stories so varied that it is not possible to pick one Domain to fit the whole genre. These include

- Genres Defined Only By Its Target Audience:

  - *Family Appeal Stories*

  - *Children/Juvenile Movies*

- Genres Described By Its Backdrop:

  - *Sport Films*

  - *Historical Pieces*

  - *Musicals*

- Reality Genres:

  - *Documentaries*

  - *Docudramas*

  - *Biographies*

The key here is to focus on our own story and determine the Domain on its own.

That's some guidance on genres and the Dramatica Domains—but we must keep in mind that genres evolve and step into new territories every day. We can start with the suggested Domains and then try something fresh *(a Situation Domain* to add terror to our **Mystery**, a *Fixed Attitude Domain* to add social depth to our **Police Story**). We must know our genre and then renew it with our screenplay—our movie deserves it.

We have nearly enough elements to complete a storyform. Now, let's try to evaluate it, to see if it's the story we really want to write or how we could change it to get it right.

APPENDIX D
GENRE AND THE EVENT ORDER FACTOR

We have worked a story through Dramatica and found the perfect structure. We have created beautiful illustrations for each story point and have a full understanding of the building blocks of our story. A question pops in our minds:

How do we turn all of this into a "real" story?

Writers throughout the ages have made statements about this obscure art of turning notes and sketches into fluid narrative—"It's like stringing beads into a necklace," some say, or "It's like weaving dozens of colorful threads in a three-dimensional loom." But apart from these poetic metaphors, we writers have few notions of how to find the proper order for our story events and appreciations. This makes each story unique and irreplaceable, and here the writer is led mostly by his personal taste, his literary culture, and of course, an exhaustive method of trial-and-error and intuition.

Still, some guidelines exist. Genre shapes a lot of them. Since the audience wants to know what sort of movie they're watching as early as possible, and needs key events at key moments to be always sure, each genre has established its own set of rules for the events' order. Most of these rules are flexible and reinvent themselves every day, but some factors are awfully strict. The audience won't forgive a Slasher film that doesn't start off with a gruesome murder.

The best way to learn the event order rules for each genre is to watch and analyze as many films as possible in that category. However, to get us started, here's a list of broad principles about the event order factor for the most popular genres:

Genres That Emphasize Actions

These include *Action Stories, Adventure Stories, Disaster Movies, Road Movies, Spy Films, Police Stories, Prison Movies, Crime Movies* and *Capers*. All of these highlight actions by putting them up front. Their first Scene is usually an exposition of the *Story Driver*, like the battle to capture Princess Leia in STAR WARS illustrates an *Action* driver. The Overall Story's Signpost 1 and Journey 1 are usually presented first in Act I, like the first chase in THE MATRIX. Acts II and III usually start with increasingly explosive depictions of the *Story Driver*, like the killings of Luke's family in Act II of STAR WARS and Obi-Wan's death in Act III. The OS events usually close those Acts to give them strong, exciting climaxes, like the battles with the forces of Sauron in LORD OF THE RINGS, THE FELLOWSHIP OF THE RING. These genres typically end with a big, Overall Story's final Signpost skirmish, such as that found in the *"Opening the Ark"* scene in RAIDERS OF THE LOST ARK. Sometimes that's followed by a conclusion of the Subjective Story thread, like the reunion between Colonel Trautman and John Rambo in FIRST BLOOD. Of course, event order is only one of the variables that identifies this genre; the actions must be huge and spectacular. Just what the audience expects.

Genres That Emphasize Suspense

These are **Thrillers, Mysteries, Whodunits, Detective Stories, Film-Noirs,** and **Suspense Movies** in general. Just as the **Action** genres work by sticking the *Story Drivers* and OS story points up front, **Suspense** genres work by hiding them. **Suspense** genres place them between acts and give them as little emphasis as possible until the end of Act III. That's when the cat comes out of the bag and the final piece shows the audience how those hidden *Drivers* and OS material actually affected the story. There are two ways to hide these events. One way is by suppressing them almost completely and letting them all out suddenly, like in CHINATOWN. The other is by placing several misleading events throughout the picture and revealing the truth in the last sequence, like in THE USUAL SUSPECTS. Either way, the key is weaving the rest of the story points naturally, as if none of them were missing, and then staging a surprising but logical reversal with the hidden elements.

Genres That Emphasize Shock

Slasher Movies, Gore, Gothic, Supernatural, Uncanny and **Horror** in general. **Horror** has a strict event order that hasn't changed much from 1931's FRANKENSTEIN to 2001's JEEPERS CREEPERS. It usually starts with a scary scene that doesn't have much to do with the rest of the plot, but sets up Genre. From here, the movie presents an Overall Story sequence that shows the characters unaware of the dangers that are about to befall them. The Main Character is presented and portrayed as a potential victim. The Impact Character—who usually turns out to be the villain—is introduced here and the first Act closes with the MC/IC relationship and the first attempt of the Villain to kill the Main Character. This arrangement is essentially repeated throughout the three acts and ends with the Villain getting destroyed in the last sequence—though leaving a door open for a sequel. In modern horror, the villain often comes back from the grave in a final

Scene and, in turn, destroys the Main Character. This sets up the first Scene of the sequel.

Though repetitive, this event order works, and audiences won't easily accept changes to it. Only hybrid *Shock Genres* (like the *Horror/Mystery* PSYCHO or the *Horror/Psycho Thriller* SILENCE OF THE LAMBS) can successfully break this strict order.

Genres That Tell A Story Through Music

Musicals *of all kinds*. These films also have a strict event order that hasn't changed much since the 18th Century operas and has continued to today's stories. Clear examples can be seen in almost any musical, from LITTLE SHOP OF HORRORS to CHICAGO. They usually start with a big number that introduces all the characters and shows the beginning of the Overall Story. Then the Main Character steps forward and presents his own tale with a song. The Impact Character appears, and her impact is felt in another solo, and the beginning of their relationship is disclosed in a duo. This order (OS, MC, IC, SS) is repeated throughout the second Act, but it's reversed in the third act (MC, IC, SS, OS). This allows a climax Scene in the Main/Impact final sequence that leads it to the final big number with all the characters and the conclusion of the Overall Story.

Humor Genres

Comedies of all kinds: *Farces, Parodies, Satires, Slapstick, Dark Humor, Situation Comedies, Fantastic Comedies, Broad-Gag Stories*. Most of these rely on the central, funny character and his interaction with the normal, everyday world. So the Main Character—in his hilarious throughline—is presented first and foremost in each act, like Woody Allen's character in ANNIE HALL and in most of Woody Allen's movies. Some *Buddy-Comedies* (like REVENGE OF THE NERDS) present the Main Character first, then the Impact Character, and then their struggle against the world. The exception to this order arrangement may be the *Parody* (like the mockumentary ZELIG) that starts with an accurate portrayal of the format and world it's about to ridicule, and then throws in the sidesplitting character to do so.

Romance Genres

Love Stories, Romantic Comedies and *Erotica*. These work by presenting the Central Characters first—their compatible personalities, their love needs, and the reasons they should belong together. Then they present the conflicting surroundings that keep them apart and the troubled relationship that results from it (like in SLEEPLESS IN SEATTLE). So a typical First Act has a Sequence about the Main Character, then one about the Impact Character, then the Overall Story, and then the Subjective Story. This succession essentially is repeated in every Act.

The array remains even though many *Romantic Comedies* work in a seemingly opposite direction. This is done by showing two incompatible characters and then introducing a converging environment that keeps them together until they fall in love, like the mismatched couple in MAID IN MANHATTAN.

Buddy Genres

In terms of event order, films make a categorical difference between love and friendship. Most *Buddy Pictures* and *Road/Buddy Pictures* present first the Environment that keeps the characters together, and then describe their opposing natures (like in 48 HRS). A typical Act starts with an OS Sequence, then the Main Character's, the Impact Character's, and the Subjective Story's to close. *Buddy* genres resemble *Action* genres in composition and tone. It's good to have this in mind when weaving a *Buddy Picture*.

Genres That Focus On A Social Problem

All kinds of *Social Dramas, Classroom Dramas, Courtroom Dramas, Business Dramas, Modern Epics, Anti-War Stories, Psycho Dramas, Domestic Dramas* and *Holocaust Dramas*. All of these strive to give an objective view of the problem, so they start with an Overall Story Sequence that shows how the problem affects all the characters. Then they continue with the rest of the throughlines that work as different views on the way to solve the central problem, like in TAXI DRIVER or BOYZ N THE HOOD. The second and third acts have a different structure, usually closing with an Overall Story Sequence that shows how the problem keeps on developing.

After the climax, a final sequence reproduces the OS-MC-IC-SS pattern in short Scenes, like TAXI DRIVER's final sequence; scenes first showing how the solutions affected the overall problem and then the toll they took on each of the characters.

Genres That Focus On A Personal Problem

The **"Education Plot" Drama,** the **"Disillusionment Plot" Drama,** the **"Redemption Plot" Drama,** the **"Punitive Plot" Drama,** the **"Testing Plot" Drama** and most **"Coming Of Age" Stories.** These films clearly need to show the Main Character perspective on life, so they start with a sequence about his status quo and attitude, such as REBEL WITHOUT A CAUSE. Many times this first sequence uses a voice-over to make the point stronger, like in AMERICAN BEAUTY.

From the first sequence on, the rest of the act shows how the Main Character's personal problem extends until it affects everyone in the story and creates grating relationships between them. So an MC, OS, IC, SS sequence order is common.

Similar to the **Social Drama** genres, the **Personal Dramas** have a Sequence of short Scenes after the climax that shows the toll that solving the problem took on everyone. It is common to find a character losing his life while solving the problem, as Plato does in REBEL WITHOUT A CAUSE, and Lester Burnham in AMERICAN BEAUTY. Most of them recognize that this death is a worthy, noble sacrifice that heals this affected soul.

Genres That Use Real World Events As A Topic

All the **Reality Genres: Documentaries, Docudramas, Biographies** and so on. These genres try to give objective and accurate views of real world problems. So they work by overemphasizing the Overall Story—presenting all the possible views on the problem—and also by giving the problem's protagonist the subjective role of Impact Character, like in Lucia Small's documentary MY FATHER, THE GENIUS. This way the audience won't identify with him and instead will adopt the view of the filmmaker—who assumes the role of Main Character by default.

This unique arrangement of the **Reality** genres is usually OS, IC, MC, SS in the first two acts and IC, MC, SS OS in the third, ending it all with the Overall Story to sum up the topic's ramifications and its general development.

Genres With Extraordinary Settings

Fantasy Stories, Science Fiction Stories, Westerns, Historical Pieces, some War Films and **Sport Films**. The "hook" for many of these movies is the astonishing and attractive sceneries for the story. So while all of them borrow their event order from another genre, they all make sure their early sequences show an inclusive panorama of that remarkable background in all its splendor. For example, LORD OF THE RINGS has a typical **Action Film** order, and BLADE RUNNER is arranged like a typical **Detective Story**.

One trick is to start off by showing the Main Character in his conventional and unattractive personal world, like the early scenes in Korben Dallas's apartment in THE FIFTH ELEMENT. Then suddenly plunge him into the unbelievable, exhilarating world outside his door.

Family Genres

Children, Juvenile and *Family Appeal* movies. The event order in this group of stories is much more diverse and less tied to genre conventions. However, they all have a strong emphasis on the Main Character to get the audience to identify with his childlike perspective, such as TOY STORY. So starting each Act with a Main Character sequence is not uncommon. Sometimes this begins as early as in the titles, also like in TOY STORY.

Exceptions to the guidelines listed above are common and are what make each movie special.

This guide, however, gives us a quick start and an early idea on how to order the material for an initial outline or first draft. From there comes a lengthy—but awfully fun—process of finding the correct order of events for our story. Find each story's own coherence and the arrangement that makes it unique.

And now that we have our Scenes in order, let's see how to structure each of them internally.

APPENDIX E

STORYFORM SETTINGS
FOR EXAMPLES IN THIS BOOK

In order to help the reader understand the Dramatica concept of story wholeness, most of the examples in this book have been taken from stories with complete storyforms and fully built characters.

The choices for the *12 Essential Questions* needed to arrive at each storyform are included in boxes near its respective examples, as are the Character Elements in the examples about Building Characters.

This allows the reader to go to the software, dial the complete Storyform and envision the appreciations that are not exposed in the example—to complete the story in his or her head and see how each of the techniques in this book works on a complete story.

CHAPTERS 1, 2 and 3:

The examples in these chapters don't include Storyforms.

CHAPTERS 4, 5 and 6:

The examples in these chapters are too partial to determine a Storyform.

CHAPTER 7:

Example 1 (**Horror Story** *about a haunted house*)

MC Resolve:	Change
MC Growth:	Stop
MC Approach:	Do-er
MC Mental Sex:	Female
OS Driver:	Decision
OS Limit:	Timelock
OS Outcome:	Success
OS Judgment:	Good
OS Domain:	Situation
OS Concern:	Future
OS Issue:	Openness
OS Problem:	Consider

Example 2 (**Courtroom Drama** *about a woman unjustly accessed of murder*)

MC Resolve:	Change
MC Growth:	Stop
MC Approach:	Be-er
MC Mental Sex:	Female
OS Driver:	Action
OS Limit:	Optionlock
OS Outcome:	Failure
OS Judgment:	Bad
OS Domain:	Fixed Attitude
OS Concern:	Conscious
OS Issue:	Appraisal
OS Problem:	Protection

Example 3 (***Action/Historical Drama*** *about the Hindenburg disaster*)

MC Resolve: .... Steadfast
MC Growth: .... Stop
MC Approach: ..... Do-er
MC Mental Sex: .. Male
OS Driver: .... Decision
OS Limit: .... Optionlock
OS Outcome: ...... Success
OS Judgment: ..... Good
OS Domain: .... Activities
OS Concern: .... Obtaining
OS Issue: .... Attitude
OS Problem: .... Support

CHAPTER 8:

Example (***Romantic Comedy*** *about a guy who falls in love with a girl passing by on a bus*)

MC Resolve: .... Change
MC Growth: .... Start
MC Approach: ..... Do-er
MC Mental Sex: .. Male
OS Driver: .... Action
OS Limit: .... Optionlock
OS Outcome: ...... Success
OS Judgment: ..... Good
OS Domain: .... Manipulation
OS Concern: ------ Developing a
                          Plan
OS Issue: .... Circumstances
OS Problem: .... Aware

CHAPTER 9:

Character Example (*Johnny*)

Motivations: ------- Feeling
                            Oppose
Methodologies: --- Production
                            Evaluation
Evaluation: ------- Ending
                            Trust
Purposes: ---------- Actuality
                            Aware

CHAPTER 10:

The examples in this chapter don't include Storyforms or Character Build Elements.

CHAPTER 11:

Character Example 1 (*Jane*)

Motivations: ------- Temptation
                            Pursuit
Methodologies: --- Reevaluation
                            Possibility
Evaluations: ------- Effect
Purposes: ---------- Desire

Character Example 2 (*Fred*)

Motivations: ------- Conscience
                            Disbelief
Methodologies: --- Evaluation
                            Probability
Evaluations: ------- Accurate
Purposes: ---------- Projection

Character Example 3 (*Mike*)

Motivations: ------- Uncontrolled
                            Avoidance
Methodologies: --- Proaction
Evaluations: ------- Cause
Purposes: ---------- Ability

Character Example 4 (*Susan*)

Motivations: ------- Control
                            Faith
Methodologies: --- Reaction
Evaluations: ------- Non-Accurate
Purposes: ---------- Speculation

These characters play into the following Storyform:

MC Resolve: .... Change
MC Growth: .... Start
MC Approach: ..... Do-er
MC Mental Sex: .. Female
OS Driver: .... Decision

OS Limit: .... Optionlock
OS Outcome: ...... Success
OS Judgment: ..... Bad
OS Domain: .... Manipulation
OS Concern: .... Playing a Role
OS Issue: .... Ability
OS Problem: .... Effect

CHAPTER 12:

Character Example 1 (*Suze*)

Motivations: ------- Consider
                     Disbelief
Methodologies: --- Proaction
                     Reevaluation
Evaluations: ------- Test
                     Determination
Purposes: ---------- Desire
Chaos

Character Example 2 (*Lt. Washington*)

Motivations: ------- Reconsider
                     Conscience
Methodologies: --- Protection
                     Nonacceptance
Evaluations: ------- Effect
                     Non-accurate
Purposes: ---------- Thought
                     Order

These characters play into the following
Storyform:

MC Resolve: .... Change
MC Growth: .... Start
MC Approach: ..... Be-er
MC Mental Sex: .. Male
OS Driver: .... Action
OS Limit: .... Optionlock
OS Outcome: ...... Success
OS Judgment: ..... Good
OS Domain: .... Activities
OS Concern: .... Obtaining
OS Issue: .... Morality
OS Problem: .... Conscience

CHAPTER 13:

Character Example 1 (*Julio*)

Motivations: ------- Consider
                     Feeling
Methodologies: --- Proaction
Evaluations: ------- Ending
Purposes: ---------- Self-Aware
                     Equity

Character Example 2 (*Raoul*)

Motivations: ------- Reconsider
                     Control
Methodologies: --- Reaction
Evaluations: ------- Unending
Purposes: ---------- Ability
                     Inequity

These characters play into the following
Storyform:

MC Resolve: .... Change
MC Growth: .... Stop
MC Approach: ..... Do-er
MC Mental Sex: .. Male
OS Driver: .... Action
OS Limit: .... Timelock
OS Outcome: ...... Failure
OS Judgment: ..... Good
OS Domain: .... Situation
OS Concern: .... Progress
OS Issue: .... Security
OS Problem: .... Process

CHAPTER 14:

Example (*Spy Thriller/Drama about
an American spy in post-communist
Russia*)

MC Resolve: .... Change
MC Growth: .... Stop
MC Approach: ..... Do-er
MC Mental Sex: .. Female
OS Driver: .... Action
OS Limit: .... Optionlock
OS Outcome: ...... Failure
OS Judgment: ..... Good

OS Domain: .... Activities
OS Concern: .... Learning
OS Issue: .... Strategy
OS Problem: .... Protection

CHAPTER 15:

Example (***SciFi/Adventure/Dark Comedy*** *about Reality-TV replacing reality*)

MC Resolve: .... Change
MC Growth: .... Stop
MC Approach: ..... Do-er
MC Mental Sex: .. Male
OS Driver: .... Action
OS Limit: .... Optionlock
OS Outcome: ...... Success
OS Judgment: ..... Bad
OS Domain: .... Activities
OS Concern: .... Obtaining
OS Issue: .... Self-interest
OS Problem: .... Pursuit

CHAPTER 16:

Example (***Mystery/Psycho Thriller/ Drama*** *storyform of the "first draft"*)

MC Resolve: .... Steadfast
MC Growth: .... Stop
MC Approach: ..... Do-er
MC Mental Sex: .. --
OS Driver: .... Action
OS Limit: .... --
OS Outcome: ...... Success
OS Judgment: ..... Bad
OS Domain: .... Activities
OS Concern: .... Learning
OS Issue: .... --
OS Problem: .... --

Storyform of the "final draft"

MC Resolve: .... Steadfast
MC Growth: .... Start
MC Approach: ..... Do-er
MC Mental Sex: .. Female
OS Driver: .... Action
OS Limit: .... Optionlock

OS Outcome: ...... Success
OS Judgment: ..... Bad
OS Domain: .... Manipulation
OS Concern: .... Conceptualizing
OS Issue: .... Situation
OS Problem: .... Perception

CHAPTER 17:

The examples in this chapter don't include Storyforms.

CHAPTER 18:

Example (*Terrorist's message unintentionally left in the guy's answering machine*)

MC Resolve: .... Steadfast
MC Growth: .... Stop
MC Approach: ..... Do-er
MC Mental Sex: .. Male
OS Driver: .... Action
OS Limit: .... Optionlock
OS Outcome: ...... Success
OS Judgment: ..... Good
OS Domain: .... Activities
OS Concern: .... Obtaining
OS Issue: .... Approach
OS Problem: .... Consider

CHAPTER 19:

The examples in this chapter don't include Storyforms.

CHAPTER 20:

Example (*The Legend about the lodge near the Wilsons' new summer cottage*)

MC Resolve: .... Change
MC Growth: .... Stop
MC Approach: ..... Do-er
MC Mental Sex: .. Female
OS Driver: .... Action
OS Limit: .... Optionlock

OS Outcome: ...... Success
OS Judgment: ..... Good
OS Domain: .... Situation
OS Concern: .... Present
OS Issue: .... Attraction
OS Problem: .... Acceptance

CHAPTER 21:

Example (A *SciFi/Social Drama/Satire* *about personal computers suddenly start to develop a soul*)

MC Resolve: .... Change
MC Growth: .... Start
MC Approach: ..... Be-er
MC Mental Sex: .. Logical
OS Driver: .... Action
OS Limit: .... Optionlock
OS Outcome: ...... Failure
OS Judgment: ..... Bad
OS Domain: .... Activity
OS Concern: .... Understanding
OS Issue: .... Interpretation
OS Problem: .... Equity

CHAPTER 22:

Example (*Docudrama* *about a stepmother accused of molesting her stepchildren*)

MC Resolve: .... Change
MC Growth: .... Stop
MC Approach: ..... Be-er
MC Mental Sex: .. Male
OS Driver: .... Action
OS Limit: .... Optionlock
OS Outcome: ...... Failure
OS Judgment: ..... Bad
OS Domain: .... Fixed Attitude
OS Concern: ------ Innermost
                    Desires
OS Issue: .... Dream
OS Problem: .... Disbelief

CHAPTER 23:

The examples in this chapter don't include Storyforms.

CHAPTER 24:

Example (*Gothic Story* *about a girl who discovers she's the heir of an ancient race of vampires*)

MC Resolve: .... Steadfast
MC Growth: .... Stop
MC Approach: ..... Do-er
MC Mental Sex: .. Female
OS Driver: .... Action
OS Limit: .... Optionlock
OS Outcome: ...... Success
OS Judgment: ..... Good
OS Domain: .... Activities
OS Concern: .... Understanding
OS Issue: .... Instinct
OS Problem: .... Ability

CHAPTER 25:

The examples in this chapter are too partial to determine a Storyform.

CHAPTER 26:

Example 1 (*Story about a serial killer and the activities to stop his endless chain of slayings*)

MC Resolve: .... Steadfast
MC Growth: .... Start
MC Approach: ..... Be-er
MC Mental Sex: .. Male
OS Driver: .... Decision
OS Limit: .... Optionlock
OS Outcome: ...... Success
OS Judgment: ..... Bad
OS Domain: .... Activities
OS Concern: .... Doing
OS Issue: .... Enlightenment
OS Problem: .... Unending

Example 2 (*A **Caper** about an operation to steal the world's most heavily guarded diamond*)

MC Resolve: .... Steadfast
MC Growth: .... Stop
MC Approach: ..... Do-er
MC Mental Sex: .. Male
OS Driver: .... Action
OS Limit: .... Optionlock
OS Outcome: ...... Success
OS Judgment: ..... Good
OS Domain: .... Activities
OS Concern: .... Obtaining
OS Issue: .... Self-interest
OS Problem: .... Avoidance

Example 3 (***Thriller/Drama*** about a widow who feels she's loosing her last chance for love)

MC Resolve: .... Change
MC Growth: .... Stop
MC Approach: ..... Do-er
MC Mental Sex: .. Female
OS Driver: .... Decision
OS Limit: .... Optionlock
OS Outcome: ...... Failure
OS Judgment: ..... Good
OS Domain: .... Activities
OS Concern: .... Obtaining
OS Issue: .... Approach
OS Problem: .... Feeling

CHAPTERS 27, 28 and 29:

The examples in these chapters are too partial to determine a Storyform.

CHAPTER 30:

The examples in this chapter don't include Storyforms.

APPENDIX F
DRAMATICA TERMINOLOGY

Dramatica is filled with specific terminology. Some of it is unique to Dramatica. Most of it consists of familiar terms used in specific, non-traditional ways. Over the years there have been changes in some of the Dramatica terminology. If you are new to Dramatica, you won't notice these changes. This appendix is limited to brief definitions. Longer definitions may be found online at Dramatica.com, in the online dictionary in the Dramatica Pro software, and in the tenth anniversary edition of *Dramatica: A New Theory of Story*.

Ability • being suited to handle a task; the innate capacity to do or be

Acceptance • a decision not to oppose

Accurate • being within tolerances

Act • an Act is a noticeable division in the dramatic flow of a story which is created by the convergence of the elements of Character, Theme, and Plot.

Action • Actions precipitate the progression of the plot

Activity • an enterprise, an initiative, an endeavor, an operation • *same as Physics*

Actuality • an objective reality — the way things are

Analysis • evaluation of the situation and/or circumstances

Antagonist • An Archetype who represents the motivations of Reconsider and Avoid/Prevent

Appraisal • an initial understanding

Appreciations • Commonly shared dramatic concepts • *same as Story Points*

Approach • The Main Character's preferred method of general problem solving

Approach • one's methodology of doing or being

Attempt • applying oneself to something not known to be within one's ability

Attitude • one's demeanor while doing or being

Attraction • drawing or being drawn to something

Avoid • stepping around, preventing or escaping from a problem rather than solving it

Aware • being conscious of things outside oneself

Bad • The Main Character ultimately fails in resolving his personal problems

Be-er • The Main Character prefers to adapt himself to his environment

Becoming • transforming one's nature • *same as Changing One's Nature*

Being • temporarily adopting a lifestyle • *same as Playing A Role*

Benchmark • the indicator of the depth of a throughline's difficulties

Catalyst • The item whose presence always pushes the story forward toward the climax

Cause • the specific circumstances that lead to an effect

Certainty • a conclusion that something is absolutely true

Change • The Main Character changes his essential nature while attempting to solve his problems

Change • an alteration of a state or process

Changing One's Nature • transforming one's nature • *same as Becoming*

Chaos • random change or a lack of order

Choice • making a decision

Circumstances • the relationship of oneself to the environment

Closure • bringing something to an end

Commitment • a decision to stick with something regardless of the consequences

Conceiving An Idea (Conceiving)• coming up with an idea

Conceptualizing • visualizing how an idea might be implemented • *same as Developing A Plan*

Concern • the goal or purpose sought after

Conditioning • responses based on experience or training

Confidence • belief in the accuracy of an expectation

Conscience • forgoing an immediate benefit because of future consequences

Conscious • considerations • *same as Contemplation*

Consequence • The area that best describes the result of failing to achieve the goal

Consider • weighing pros and cons

Contagonist • An Archetype representing the motivations of temptation and hinder

Contemplation • considerations • *same as Conscious*

Control • a method based on organization and constraint

Cost • the price that must be paid while meeting the requirements of the goal

Critical Flaw • The Character trait that inhibits the effectiveness of that Character's Unique Ability

Decision • decisions force actions; decisions precipitate the progression of the plot

Deduction • a process of thought that determines certainty

Deficiency • motivation based on lack

Delay • putting off until later

Denial • the refusal to let something go

Desire • the motivation to change one's situation or circumstances

Destiny • the future path an individual will take

Determination • a conclusion about the cause behind a particular effect

Developing A Plan • visualizing how an idea might be implemented • *same as Conceptualizing*

Direction • The way a character grows in his attempt to solve his problems, toward either "Start" or "Stop" • *same as Growth*

Disbelief • the belief that something is untrue

Dividend • the benefits gathered while meeting the requirements of the goal

Do-er • As an approach, the Main Character prefers to adapt his environment to himself

Doing • engaging in a physical activity

Domain • The broadest area in which a problem can be found, *e.g. Situation, Fixed Attitude, Activities, and Manipulation*

Doubt • questioning validity without investigating to be sure

Dream • a desired future that requires unexpected developments

Driver • the kind of activity focused on in the effort to solve the story's problem • *same as Story Driver*

Effect • the specific outcome forced by a cause

Emotion • An Archetype who represents the motivations of Feeling and Uncontrolled

Empathy • Empathy describes the complete identification of the audience with the Main Character such that the audience sees the story through his eyes.

Ending • coming to a conclusion

Enlightenment • an understanding that transcends knowledge •

Equity • a balance, fairness, or stability

Evaluation • an appraisal of a situation and/or circumstances

Evidence • information supporting a belief

Expectation • a conclusion as to the eventual effect of a particular cause

Expediency • most efficient course considering repercussions

Experience • the gaining of familiarity

Fact • belief in something real

Failure • the original goal is not achieved

Faith • accepting something as certain without proof

Falsehood • that which has been shown to be erroneous

Fantasy • belief in something unreal

Fate • a future situation that will befall an individual

Feeling • an emotional sense of how things are going

Female Mental Sex • The Main Character uses female problem solving techniques • *same as Intuitive (Holistic) Problem Solving Style*

Fixed Attitude • a fixed attitude, fixation, or bias • *same as Mind*

Forewarnings • the indications that the consequence is growing more imminent

Future • what will happen or what will be

Gathering Information • gathering information or experience • *same as Learning*

Goal • the central objective of a story

Good • If at the end of the story the Main Character is no longer nagged by his personal problems, the judgment of the story can be said to be Good

Grand Argument Story • A story that illustrates all four throughlines (Overall Story, Subjective Story, Main Character, and Impact Character) in their every appreciation so that no holes are left in either the passionate or dispassionate arguments of that story

Growth • The way a character grows in his attempt to solve his problems, toward either "Start" or "Stop"

Guardian • An archetype that represents the motivations of Conscience and Help

Help • a direct assistance to another's effort to achieve their goal

Hinder • a direct detraction from another's effort to achieve their goal

Holistic or Intuitive • The Main Character uses female problem solving techniques • *same as Female Mental Sex*

Hope • a desired future if things go as expected

How Things Are Going • the way things are progressing

Hunch • a conclusion based on intuition

Impact Character • The Character that forces the Main Character to face his personal problem

Impact Character's Critical Flaw • The item that undermines the Impact Character's efforts

Impact Character's Problem • The source of the Impact Character's drive

Impact Character's Solution • what is needed to truly satisfy The Impact Character's motivation

Impact Character's Throughline • The broadest description of the Impact Character's impact in a specific story

Impact Character's Unique Ability • The item that makes the Impact Character uniquely able to thwart the Main Character

Impulsive Responses • immediate responses • *same as Preconscious*

Inaction • taking no action as a means of response

Induction • a means of determining possibility

Inequity • an unbalance, unfairness, or lack or stability

Inertia • a continuation of a state or process

Innermost Desires • basic drives and desires • *same as Subconscious*

Instinct • intrinsic unconditioned responses

Interdiction • an effort to change a predetermined course

Interpretation • determination of possible meaning

Intuitive or Holistic • The Main Character uses female problem solving techniques • *same as Female Mental Sex*

Investigation • gathering evidence to resolve questions of validity

Issue • The thematic meaning of the Throughline being explored

Judgment • The author's assessment of whether or not the Main Character has resolved his personal problem

Knowledge • that which one holds to be true

Leap of Faith • Having run out of time or options and come to the moment of truth, the Main Character decides to either Change or remain Steadfast with no way of knowing which will best lead him to his goal or resolve his personal problem

Learning • gathering information or experience

Limit • The restricted amount of time or options that, by running out, forces the story to a climax

Linear or Logical • The Main Character uses male problem solving techniques • *same as Male Mental Sex*

Logic • a rational sense of how things are related

Main Character • A story has a central character that acts as the focus of the audience's emotional attachment to the story. This Main Character is the conduit through whom the audience experiences the story subjectively.

Main Character's Concern • The Main Character's personal objective or purpose, the area of the Main Character's concern

Main Character's Critical Flaw • the quality that undermines The Main Character's efforts

Main Character Problem • source of The Main Character's motivation; the source of the Main Character's problems

Main Character's Solution • what is needed to truly satisfy The Main Character's motivation; the solution to the Main Character's problems

Main Character's Throughline • the general area in which The Main Character operates

Main Character's Unique Ability • the quality that makes The Main Character uniquely qualified to solve the story's problem/achieve the goal

Male Mental Sex • The Main Character uses male problem solving techniques

Manipulation • a manner of thinking • *same as Psychology*

Memory • recollections

Mental Sex • a determination of the Main Character's mental operating system • *same as Problem Solving Style*

Methodology • the elements a character will implement to achieve his Purposes

Mind • a fixed attitude • *same as Fixed Attitude*

Morality • doing or being based on what is best for others

Motivation • The elements that represent the drives behind a character's Purposes

Need • that which is required

Non-Acceptance • a decision to oppose

Non-Accurate • not within tolerances

Overall Story Concern • The area of concern in the objective story • *see Concern.*

Overall Story Consequence • The area that best describes the result of failing to achieve the goal • *see Consequence.*

Overall Story Costs • The area that best describes the costs incurred while trying to achieve the goal • *see Costs.*

Overall Story Dividends • The area that best describes the dividends accrued while trying to achieve the goal • *see Dividends.*

Overall Story Forewarnings • The area that best describes the imminent approach of the story consequences • *see Forewarnings.*

Overall Story Goal • The common goal of the objective characters • *see Goal.*

Overall Story Preconditions • The area that best describes the conditions imposed on meeting the story's requirements • *see Preconditions.*

Overall Story Prerequisites • The area that best describes what is needed to meet the story requirements • *see Prerequisites.*

Overall Story Problem • The source of the objective story's problems • *see Problem*

Overall Story Requirements • The area that best describes the requirements that must be met prior to achieving the goal • *see Requirements.*

Overall Story Solution • The solution to the objective story's problems

Overall Story Throughline • The domain in which the objective story takes place

Obligation • accepting a task or situation in exchange for someone's potential favors

Obtaining • achieving or possessing something

Openness • willingness to reevaluate

Oppose • an indirect detraction from another's effort

Optionlock • the story climax occurs because all other options have been exhausted

Order • an arrangement in which patterns are seen

Outcome • an assessment of how things ended up

Past • what has already happened

Perception • the way things seem to be

Permission • one's ability based on what is allowed

Physics • an activity • *same as Activity*

Playing A Role • temporarily adopting a lifestyle • *same as Being*

Possibility • a determination that something might be true

Potentiality • a determination that something has the capacity to become true

Preconception • unwillingness to reevaluate

Preconditions • limitations tacked on to an effort

Preconscious • immediate responses • *same as Impulsive Responses*

Prediction • a determination of a future state of affairs

Prerequisites • preliminary steps that must be met

Present • the current situation and circumstances

Proaction • taking initiative action to achieve one's goals

Probability • a determination of likelihood

Problem • the underlying cause of the story's difficulties

Problem-Solving Style • a determination of the Main Character's mental operating system • *same as Mental Sex*

Process • the mechanism through which a cause leads to an effect

Production • a process of thought that determines potential

Progress • the way things are going • *same as How Things Are Going*

Projection • an extension of probability into the future

Protagonist • An archetype who represents the motivations of Pursuit and Consider

Protection • an effort to prevent one's concerns from being vulnerable to interference

Proven • a rating of knowledge based on corroboration

Psychology • a manner of thinking • *same as Manipulation*

Purpose • The intentions which any character has in a story

Pursuit • a directed effort to resolve a problem

Rationalization • a logical alternative used to mask the real reason

Reaction • actions made in response

Reappraisal • a reconsideration of a conclusion

Reason • An Archetype who represents the motivations of Logic and Control

Reconsider • questioning a conclusion based on additional information

Reduction • a process of thought that determines probability

Reevaluation • a reappraisal of a situation or circumstances

Repulsion • pushing or being pushed away from

Requirements • the necessary precursor to achieving the goal

Resolve • the degree to which the Main Character feels compelled to remain on the quest

Responsibility • the belief that one is best suited to accomplish a task

Result • the ramifications of a specific effect

Security • an evaluation of one's protections

Self-Aware • being conscious of one's own existence

Self Interest • doing or being based on what is best for oneself

Sense of Self • one's perception of oneself

Senses • sensory observations

Sidekick • An Archetype who represents the motivations of Faith and Support

Situation • a situation • *same as Universe*

Situation • the arrangement of one's environment

Skeptic • An Archetypal Character possessing the qualities of disbelief and oppose

Skill • practiced ability

Solution • the specific element needed to resolve the story's problem

Speculation • an extension of possibility into the future

Start • The audience wants something in the story, which is directly connected to the Main Character, to begin

State of Being • one's true self

Steadfast • The Main Character sticks with his essential nature while attempting to solve the problem

Stop • The audience wants something in the story, which is directly connected to the Main Character, to desist

Story Mind • The central concept from which Dramatica was derived is the notion of the Story Mind. Rather than seeing stories simply as some characters interacting, Dramatica sees the entire story as an analogy to a single human mind dealing with a particular problem. This mind, the Story Mind, contains all the characters, themes, and plot progressions of the story as incarnations of the psychological processes of problem solving. In this way, each story *explores* the inner workings of the mind so we (as audience) may take a more objective view of our decisions and indecisions and learn from the experience.

Story Driver • the kind of activity focused on in the effort to solve the story's problem

Story Points • Commonly shared dramatic concepts • *same as Appreciations*

Storyform • The structural and dynamic skeleton of a story

Storyforming • the process of creating the dramatics of a unique story by arranging structure and dynamics

Strategy • a plan to achieve one's purpose or a plan of response

Subconscious • basic drives and desires • *same as Innermost Desires*

Subjective Story • the story as it relates to the conflict between the Main and Impact Characters • *same as Main v. Impact Story*

Subjective Story Problem • the underlying cause of the difficulties between the Main Character and the Impact Character

Subjective Story Solution • the specific element needed to resolve the difficulties between the Main Character and The Impact Character

Subjective Story Throughline • the general area in which the subjective story takes place

Subplot • An amplification of a branch or aspect of a storyform

Success • the original goal is achieved

Support • an indirect assistance given to another's efforts

Suspicion • questioning a belief based on evidence

Symptom • the principal symptom of the story problem

Temptation • the urge to embrace immediate benefits despite possible consequences

Test • a trial to determine something's validity

Theme • The author's statement about the relative worth of different value standards as they are compared in all contexts essential to the story

Theory • an unbroken chain of relationships leading from a premise to a conclusion

Thought • the process of consideration

Threat • an evaluation of one's vulnerabilities

Throughline • The sequence of story points that describe one of the four Perspectives in a story

Timelock • the story climax is forced by a time limit

Trust • an acceptance of knowledge as proven without first testing its validity

Truth • that which has been proven correct

Unending • a continuance without cessation

Uncontrolled • a disorganized response

Understanding • appreciating the meaning of something

Unique Ability • The item that makes the Main Character uniquely able to resolve the Overall Story Problem; the item that makes the Impact Character uniquely able to thwart the Main Character's efforts

Universe • a situation • *same as Situation*

Unproven • a rating of knowledge that has not been tested

Value • the objective usefulness or desirability of something in general

Wisdom • understanding how to apply Knowledge

Work • applying oneself to something known to be within one's ability

Worry • concern for the future

Worth • a rating of usefulness or desirability to oneself

INDEX

U

ABOUT THE AUTHOR

Armando Saldaña Mora (born in Mexico City, 1964) has been a professional writer since 1985. "The key to succeed in this profession," he says, "is being able to create top quality material for any genre, any format, any medium." Accordingly, his career has taken him from authoring and producing stage plays, to crafting and editing novels, to originating and redrafting screenplays, to scriptwriting and conducting writer's workshops for TV networks. "I couldn't have done all this without Dramatica," he says, "Really. What else can I say?"

If you have a question for Armando regarding *Dramatica for Screenwriters,* please send an email to: *bookquestions@write-bros.com.* Please put *"Armando Book Question"* in the Subject line. All correspondence to this email address becomes the property of Write Brothers, Inc.

Made in the USA
Lexington, KY
28 May 2011